JAN 2 2 2020

P9-BIK-616

NAPA COUNTY LIBRARY
580 COOMBS STREET
NAPA, CA 94559

MIRACLE IN LAKE PLACID

MIRACLE IN LAKE PLACID

THE GREATEST HOCKEY STORY EVER TOLD

JOHN GILBERT

SPORTS
PUBLISHING

Copyright © 2019 by John Gilbert

All rights reserved. No part of this book may be reproduced in any manner without the express written consent of the publisher, except in the case of brief excerpts in critical reviews or articles. All inquiries should be addressed to Sports Publishing, 307 West 36th Street, 11th Floor, New York, NY 10018.

Sports Publishing books may be purchased in bulk at special discounts for sales promotion, corporate gifts, fund-raising, or educational purposes. Special editions can also be created to specifications. For details, contact the Special Sales Department, Sports Publishing, 307 West 36th Street, 11th Floor, New York, NY 10018 or sportspubbooks@skyhorsepublishing.com.

Sports Publishing® is a registered trademark of Skyhorse Publishing, Inc.®, a Delaware corporation.

Visit our website at www.sportspubbooks.com.

10 9 8 7 6 5 4 3 2 1

Library of Congress Cataloging-in-Publication Data is available on file.

Cover design by Brian Peterson
Cover photo credit Getty Images

ISBN: 978-1-68358-306-6
Ebook ISBN: 978-1-68358-307-3

Printed in the United States of America

Contents

1

Never to Be Duplicated

WHENEVER AN EVENT IS DEFINED by superlatives, it's usually hyper-
bole from someone caught up in the moment. The biggest game or
the best game might only stand up until tomorrow's game, which
could be bigger or better. That is not the case with the United States
hockey team's incredible gold-medal performance in the 1980 Winter Olympics at Lake Placid, New York.

When Team USA upset the seemingly invincible Soviet Union,
4–3, then came back two days later to rally for three goals in the
third period to beat Finland, 4–2, the No. 7-seeded Team USA had
won a gold medal that captivated the whole country and shocked the
hockey-playing world.

It couldn't happen, shouldn't have happened, but it did happen because a visionary coach named Herb Brooks forced facts into his own private fantasy and nurtured it to reality. Team USA's gold medal performance in 1980 also will remain the standard by which so-called "miracles" in all other sports are rendered trite by comparison.

It can never be duplicated in the real world, or at the next Winter Olympics, or in any future Winter Olympics.

This one remains so unique that 40 years after the storybook ending, people are still talking about it and agreeing with *Sports Illustrated*'s assessment that it ranks No. 1 as the single most spectacular sports story of the twentieth century. Might as well include the twenty-first century, as well.

Sports can be all-consuming and hugely entertaining in every season. The World Series, Super Bowl, NCAA basketball tournament, Indianapolis 500, Kentucky Derby, and Masters golf tournament are annual attractions that are almost always exciting and entertaining. But there is no chance that the next World Series or Super Bowl might topple from its pinnacle what happened in Lake Placid in 1980.

The ground rules, and the ground itself, have changed so much since that Olympic tournament, there is no possible way 20 eager young collegians, hand-selected and then driven to physical and mental extremes by Brooks, a visionary coach, could be trained to somehow roll undefeated through the best European professional hockey players on the world stage.

The great Russian, Swedish, Finnish, and Czech players earned a decent living playing hockey in their respective Elite leagues back then but were considered amateurs by the International Ice Hockey Federation, while the North American pros who signed National Hockey League contracts were considered professionals. Canada, in fact, didn't participate in the 1972 or 1976 Olympics in protest of their pro players not being allowed to play. Canada returned with an amateur team not unlike the Team USA program for 1980.

In the years after 1980, the top European "amateurs" started migrating to North America, lured by multimillion-dollar contracts in the NHL. Then, in 1998, the circumstances did a 180 when the IIHF agreed to allow NHL pros to enter the Olympics, and the genie definitely escaped from the bottle.

The NHL and ABC Television's huge influence convinced the International Olympic Committee and the IIHF to change its Olympic tournament ground rules too, leaving the intricate but intense round-robin format, where any loss could preclude a medal-round chance, to switch to brackets that played down from quarterfinals to semifinals to a gold-medal final that could be followed as easily as the NCAA basketball brackets. The NHL had so many players going back to represent their countries that the NHL pretty much took over running the hockey tournament in 2002.

If NHL pros were eliminated from the Olympics, and some sort of amateur purity could be reestablished, the tournament would still never be the same.

"You can't ever duplicate it," said forward David Christian, as the 40th anniversary of that magical year approached, and it was time again to look back to the wonders that transpired in the colorful little upstate New York village of Lake Placid.

Other players agreed that it could never be repeated, and they take some satisfaction in how it continues to prevail. When apprised of the project to recapture all of the facts and some of the legends of the drama of the 1980 Olympics in this book, in time for the 40th anniversary of the event, they agreed that my private archives of notes, quotes, and details from those games at the time they happened would be preferable to asking the players to search their varying memories 40 years later.

"The whole thing is pretty vague in all our minds," laughed defenseman Billy Baker. "It all went by so fast, it was like a blur. When we get a few guys together, somebody will remember some little detail that happened in a game, and somebody else might argue it was from a different game. We all remember certain details, and when we get together, talking about it always brings back other memories.

"It was no big deal at the time, and if we'd realized how big it would become, maybe we'd have paid closer attention, or taken notes ourselves. A lot of fans don't recall it very well, either. Rammer [Mike Ramsey] and I go fishing together, and we figure we've had 10,000 or 15,000 people tell us over the years that they remember being at our game against Russia—in an arena that holds 7,100."

Ramsey suggested Baker was light on his fan count. "I've had at least 40,000 people tell me they were at that game in an arena that holds 8,100," Ramsey said, 39 years after the game.

Saving all my notes from covering the hockey tournament at Lake Placid for the *Minneapolis Tribune* makes my "archives" a valuable asset—although my wife, Joan, knows it's all part of being a packrat. In this case, however, I had the benefit of exclusive interviews with Brooks and his players after each game, which makes my packrat habit irreplaceable.

At the time, of course, I used some of those quotes to accent my game stories in the *Minneapolis Tribune* but was limited by that day's space, and what was most pertinent to that game. Some other quotes appeared in a book I wrote chronicling Brooks's coaching career titled *Herb Brooks: The Inside Story of a Hockey Mastermind*, which covered my relationship with him from before he started coaching right up through his NHL coaching days and until his untimely death at age 66 in a one-vehicle freeway rollover crash on August 11, 2003. Most of those exclusive comments from Brooks and 1980 team members, however, have never before been published. Until this book, the perfect opportunity to gather them all.

Baker and Christian, both defensemen on the 1980 US team, have a couple of indelible memories of plays that have stood up to the test of time, because they were vital parts of two of the most important goals in the US Olympic success—Baker in the first game tie against Sweden, and Christian with his contribution to the buzzer-beating tally at the end of the first period that helped stun the Soviet Union.

Of course, there were numerous other highlights, from Jim Craig's great goaltending, to Mike Eruzione's game-winning goal against the Soviet Union, to the prolific goal-scoring of Mark Johnson while playing with a separated shoulder taped so tightly through the last five games that it seemed unlikely he could shoot, to the intuitive playmaking of Mark Pavelich, and to the thumping body checks delivered by the youngest player on the team, defenseman Mike Ramsey, who was only 19.

The overriding fact, however, is that the many more subtle contributions by every player on the roster, combined with the plays that have lived in the spotlight of history, were all choreographed by the creative manipulating and strategic planning of Brooks. And it took frequent injections of good luck and maybe a little cosmic energy, shaken together into a blend that makes the term "miracle" appropriate for the unique story of what all went into the Miracle at Lake Placid.

2

1980 Needed Big 1979

THERE ARE SURPRISES, BIG AND small, every year in international hockey, but the seven-game run of surprises strung together at Lake Placid make 1980 the unlikeliest gold medal in Olympic hockey history. In the process, United States hockey was thrust to an elite status that it is not likely to ever relinquish.

Coach Herb Brooks concocted an outrageous plan, then had enough self-discipline to keep his foot on the gas and his eye on the target as he inspired his charges each step of the way. Of course, the Olympics were completed by the last week of February 1980, meaning to get to that year took something of a storybook year in 1979 to set it all up.

Brooks was venturing into uncharted territory, but he was always driven by his passionate if idealistic belief that he could select the right players for an elite team and coordinate them into a unit that could perform in a totally flexible system, right out of his imagination. Nobody else on the planet has ever been capable of even imagining such a plan. A lot of teams are capable of changing from one attacking or defending system to another, even during a game. Brooks envisioned training his players to anticipate and respond to game situations in a manner predictable only to their teammates. He called it "sophisticated pond hockey," and the beauty of his system was that it was no system and every system, all at once. Put simply, you never have to adjust if you're always adjusting.

Brooks already knew he had been selected by a somewhat reluctant Amateur Hockey Association of the US—AHAUS, which later became USA Hockey—after Harvard's Bill Cleary turned it down. That didn't interrupt his task at hand, which was coaching the University of Minnesota for the 1978–79 season, the most talented and competitive season in the Western Collegiate Hockey Association's rich history. Brooks led the Gophers through to a final-game runner-up league finish, then they went on to win their third NCAA championship in his seven years as coach. When Brooks took over the last-place Gophers, they had never won an NCAA title, and after one .500 season, he guided Minnesota to NCAA titles in 1974, 1976, and 1979.

Almost immediately after that, he assembled the 1979 US national team for what turned out to be a pretty dismal performance in the World Championships in Moscow. The US won only two games and was beaten twice by West Germany in the "B Pool" for a lowly seventh-place finish. Brooks immediately resumed what is surely the most comprehensive research and selection process ever attempted in picking a team, beginning with invitations carefully vetted by Brooks for the midsummer National Sports Festival at Colorado Springs.

After that, Brooks began installing a creative system of play that pushed his players into situations where they would be forced to use their own trained instincts to make plays in a total team concept, developed during a lengthy and competitive pre-Olympic exhibition tour of pro, college, and European opponents that went right up to the end of calendar year 1979.

Coaching at Minnesota, Brooks had a head start, because he had recruited key Olympic candidates from his own highly skilled Gophers, as well as closely observing others during multiple games against archrivals Wisconsin, North Dakota, and Minnesota-Duluth. Center Mark Johnson and defenseman Bob Suter played for Wisconsin; center Mark Pavelich and wing John Harrington played for Minnesota-Duluth; and David Christian was a star forward at North Dakota.

Brooks quite famously had been the last player cut from the 1960 US team that won its only previous gold medal in Squaw Valley, California. In the last game of the 1978–79 regular season, North Dakota beat Minnesota in the old Williams Arena in Minneapolis to win the WCHA championship when David Christian—the son of Billy Christian, Warroad, Minnesota's star of the 1960 US gold medal team—scored a hat trick. When Brooks pulled his goaltender in the final minute, David Christian rubbed it in against the old family friend by skating in alone at full speed toward the empty net, then stopping abruptly at the crease in a spray of ice chips before blasting a slapshot in to complete his hat trick.

Several weeks later, at the Detroit Olympia, Minnesota got payback of the richest kind when freshman Neal Broten scored a highlight video goal, flying through the air as he scored what proved to be the winning goal as the Gophers defeated North Dakota, 4–3, in the NCAA championship game. From that championship team, Broten joined Gophers teammates Eric Strobel, Rob McClanahan, Steve Christoff, Phil Verchota, defensemen Billy Baker and Mike Ramsey, plus goaltender Steve Janaszak as Olympic selections. Another former Gopher, Buzzy Schneider, who had played on four earlier US national teams, was the oldest player selected for the 1980 Team USA squad at age 25.

Several of those players were also on the US national team Brooks coached at the 1979 World Championships in Moscow. The US went 2–2–2 to finish third, but that was third in Group B, the second tier, behind Finland and West Germany, ahead of only winless Poland. The Soviet Union, playing at home in Moscow, won the gold, Czechoslovakia the silver, and Sweden the bronze in Group A, with properly amateur Canada fourth.

Being in Group B was grating enough, but the US lost, 6–3, to West Germany in pool play and later lost again to West Germany, 5–2, in the fifth-place game, which placed West Germany at 3–2–1 as runner-up to Finland's 4–1–1 atop Group B and dropped the US to seventh in the combined overall standings. Those standings also determined the seedings for the 1980 Winter Olympic tournament in Lake Placid, which were: 1. USSR, 2. Czechoslovakia, 3. Sweden, 4. Canada, 5. Finland, 6. West Germany, and then, 7. Team USA, followed by Poland, Holland, Romania, Norway, and Japan.

In Moscow, Brooks gained a little culture and provided a bit of lasting humor for Lou Vairo, who was a longtime coaching tactician after growing up on roller hockey in Brooklyn, became a devoted student of the Soviet tactical wizardry of Anatoli Tarasov, and later coached an Olympic team himself. Vairo hadn't known Brooks well, or even liked him, until he was invited by Brooks to come along as a special adviser on the walkie-talkie from the press box at the World Championships—a role he also filled at Lake Placid. On one night off, Vairo said he borrowed a suit coat and he and Brooks went to the Bolshoi Ballet.

"We saw *Swan Lake*," Vairo recalled. "I asked Herb if he was enjoying it, and he said, 'The dancing doesn't do much for me, but the band's pretty good.' A little while later, he fell asleep."

Vairo needed some time to learn to appreciate Brooks, but after observing him up close, he was more than just impressed. "He was a brilliant man," Vairo said. "One of the smartest people I've ever talked to. He could have been governor of Minnesota or president of the United States."

Interestingly, back in Minnesota years later, representatives from both the Democratic and Republican parties tried to recruit Brooks to run for state office. "I think they both thought I was better suited to the other party," Brooks said. "Maybe I'm a populist."

Brooks may not have become a ballet fancier in Moscow, but he gained some important insight about some of his 1980 candidates from the 1979 World Championships. Players on that team who ultimately made the Olympic team included Jim Craig in goal, Baker and Jack O'Callahan on defense, and forwards Verchota, Strobel, McClanahan, Christoff, and Mark Johnson. Several more who were ultimately late cuts from the final Olympic roster were forwards Ralph Cox and Dave Delich, and defensemen Les Auge and Jack Hughes. Craig Patrick was another wing on that 1979 team, which led him to a whole new career.

As a player, Patrick, who had played at Denver University and on several pro teams, including the Minnesota Fighting Saints, said he appreciated Brooks's free-skating offensive style. "It was refreshing to be able to move and weave like he wanted us to," said Patrick. "It was a lot of fun—great."

But partway through the tournament, Patrick's playing days ended, gracefully, when Brooks pulled him aside and offered him the chance to become his assistant coach for the Olympic team. Patrick accepted. First off, Brooks told Patrick he planned to be a real jerk to the players sometimes, and that Patrick would have to be the soft-spoken, unifying factor and friend. Sort of a good cop-bad cop deal. The players from the East and West didn't like each other, Brooks told him, "and the only way to keep them from hating each other is to make them all hate me."

That technique worked pretty well in several instances over the next year, and it wasn't until time passed afterward that the players appreciated him more with each passing year.

Every coach likes to make his team an underdog, but it didn't take much effort for Team USA. After ranking seventh and being relegated to Group B in the 1979 World Championships, Team USA was assured of being the longest of Olympic long shots. That may have relieved any undue pressure, not that it mattered to Brooks, who was too busy acquiring more input on prospects for the preparation he had in mind. One beneficiary of Brooks's talent for seeing beyond what was on the ice was Jack O'Callahan, a competitive, team-oriented defenseman from Boston University who grew up in the tough Boston suburb of Charlestown. He didn't think he had played very well at the World Championships and was sure he had played himself out of consideration. He was surprised when Brooks called and told his agent he wanted O'Callahan to come to the National Sports Festival to try for a spot on the Olympic team. O'Callahan said he was impressed that Brooks saw beyond his marginal performance in Moscow and was more focused on character and team leadership.

An inside glimpse of depth of the preparation came from Dave Brooks, Herb's younger brother, who used to identify himself as "HLB," for "Herbie's Little Brother." Dave recalled going to a family gathering at Herb and Patti Brooks's home on Turtle Lake in the Twin Cities suburb of Shoreview several months before the

1979 National Sports Festival and noting how everybody was there but Herb. Patti said Herb was down in his office, and when Dave walked in, he found Herb in the midst of making numerous phone calls to friends, coaches, teachers, and family members of the many players he was considering inviting to the festival. Mistakes can be made easily watching players in a short series, but Brooks figured that if all 70 candidates were of the highest character, then any mistakes in evaluations would still result in a quality selection.

3

Fierce Festival

THE HOCKEY TOURNAMENT AT THE National Sports Festival at the
Broadmoor World Arena in Colorado Springs in the summer of
'79 was hotly competitive, with the 70 hand-selected participants
divided onto four somewhat regional rosters. In college hockey, the
rivalry between Eastern and Western college teams was intense,
bordering on hostile. Coach Herb Brooks and his players were well
aware of that and, in fact, had played a role in heightening it when
his Gophers and Boston University engaged in a bench-clearing
brawl in the NCAA semifinals at Denver's DU Arena in 1976. The
Gophers went on to win the game and the championship. Some BU
players reportedly were still incensed about that, so creating har-

mony with those factions was always high on Coach Brooks's mind, from the evaluation process right on through the Olympic Games.

The movie *Miracle* played up that regional rivalry by having the Jack O'Callahan and Rob McClanahan characters engage in a practice fight, with O'Callahan saying it was because McClanahan was on the Minnesota team that had cost BU a possible NCAA title. In reality, that fight never happened. Others said the hassle was between O'Callahan and Steve Christoff, another Gopher. Either way, the revenge factor didn't hold water, melted or frozen. As often happens, facts get in the way of a good story: neither McClanahan nor Christoff played on the 1976 championship Gophers team, because both were still in high school—McClanahan at Mounds View and Christoff at Richfield.

Sports festivals were held every year back then, and there had been a scrap at the 1978 edition. O'Callahan recalled he fought Christoff, but identities might be obscured. Billy Baker recalled it was between O'Callahan and Greg Woods, who played at Denver. "Denver had been ineligible to go the year BU won the tournament," Baker said. "A little bad blood was left from that and came out at the 1978 Sports Festival." With Woods not making the 1980 team, there would have been no relevance for that fight to make the screenplay, so the movie guys went for the Hollywood-esque account.

To evaluate the 70 prospects at their National Sports Festival tournament, Brooks invited some trusted hockey people and also welcomed input from every NHL, minor-league pro, college, and amateur coach, manager, and scout. He listened to all of them, throughout the week, and was a master politician, listening diplomatically to every suggestion and recommendation, keeping studious notes. But he also kept a private notebook in which he compiled his own personal observations and assessments. And he showed that to no one. The idea may have germinated from his old college coach, the colorful John Mariucci, Minnesota's legendary "Godfather of Hockey," who explained that as coach, he always had the players vote for their captain. "But I counted the ballots," he'd add, with a familiar gleam in his eye.

Brooks groomed Patrick to make the transition from winger to assistant coach and assistant general manager, and from the start of the Sports Festival, Patrick saw the benefits of the organizational work Brooks had put into the process, including psychological evaluations to be filled out by each player and the physical training regimen designed by physiologist Jack Blatherwick and given to all candidates before the festival. Identified by Brooks as "Cardiac Jack," Blatherwick was physical training's version of a mad scientist. He studied every facet of physical exertion and created specialized quick-interval drills that enhanced quickness and stamina for hockey players at the University of Minnesota.

The games themselves among the four festival teams were fast-paced and very entertaining. The Broadmoor World Arena rink's unusual shape was more square, wider, and shorter than standard North American or European hockey rinks, with most of the seats on one side and at one end. The press box, opposite the main grandstand, required some agility to reach, with boards nailed to the side beams, making a ladder that reached up to a small, square opening. Carrying a typewriter and a briefcase, with some sort of transmitting device in that pre-cell phone era gave any media member a proper challenge. Brooks watched every game from that press box, too, while scattered around the arena were his trusted friends and associates on his advisory group.

Gus Hendrickson from Minnesota-Duluth coached the Midwest team of all Minnesotans; Bill Selman from St. Louis University and formerly at Minnesota-Duluth coached the Great Lakes team of players from Michigan, Wisconsin, and points west; Jerry York, who was at Bowling Green at the time, directed the Central team, with players from Minnesota and North Dakota; and Charlie Holt from the University of New Hampshire coached the New England team, made up of players mainly from Eastern colleges. Minnesota had by far the most candidates, which made sense because most colleges still depended on Canadian players, and Minnesotans were the first Americans to break through the hockey hierarchy in meaningful numbers, followed by New England and then Michigan.

Teams would play through the week, starting with a full round of games against the other regional teams, after which they would pair up 1 vs. 4 and 2 vs. 3, with the losers playing for third place and the winners for the championship. After each session, Brooks gathered his advisory staff to discuss players in the games. All the team officials stayed at the Antlers Hotel in Colorado Springs, where I also stayed with my wife, Joan, and our two sons, Jack and Jeff. We had driven there to combine a family vacation with my coverage of the event for the *Minneapolis Tribune*. I had already been assigned to go to Lake Placid to cover the US hockey team and its anticipated heavy Minnesota influence, and covering the selection process was an exciting preamble.

Through the week, I kept my usual lengthy notes on the games and individual performances, sending daily accounts to the *Minneapolis Tribune*, mostly on the many Minnesotans among the candidates, but I pretty much kept my distance from Brooks. We had become close friends both professionally and personally since he was an assistant coach at Minnesota, before becoming head coach in 1972. We also had always shared on- and off-the-record conversations about hockey, from the NHL to the high schools, and including a mutual admiration for the dominant European national teams, particularly the exceptional Soviet Union teams of that time. I knew how much Brooks admired the innovative style of

Russian play, and I knew what kind of players he liked. I also had watched as he installed several of his own regrouping tactics with his Gophers college teams, although he didn't apply them in game conditions. I teased him about preferring to watch his practices more than Gophers games because they did so many more progressive things in practice. Finally, he recruited a crop of talent that led him to deploy more puck-possession tricks on his last two Minnesota teams, including the 1979 championship Gophers.

But with all the careful planning for the Sports Festival, I realized that the team selections would be announced at a press conference right after the championship game on that final Saturday night. That meant, with the time zone differences, it would be near midnight in my Central time zone, and after midnight on the media-heavy East Coast, so nobody east of Colorado would get the news until the following day. So I devised a plan.

After compiling my own list of the 26 candidates I guessed had the best chance, I added one more name and walked down the hall to Brooks's room. With the championship game still several hours away, he invited me in, and I kidded him about being able to read his mind, then I told him the press conference would be too late to make any major newspapers, so I was writing a story for all editions of the *Minneapolis Tribune* in which I would predict the selections. He was amused, and I said I would cloak my picks in conditional language such as "it is believed Brooks will name these defensemen . . . " and so forth. I wanted to show him my list, just in case I was way off on anybody.

He said I had picked all three goaltenders correctly and that I had also gotten all eight defensemen. As he started going down my list of forwards, he paused and reached into his briefcase for his personal list. "Nobody has seen this list," he said, "and I'm just showing it to you to prove that you only missed one."

I pointed out that my mistake could be explained by the asterisk next to the name of Vermont star Craig Homola, a skilled center from Eveleth, Minnesota. At the bottom of my list, I had explained the asterisk by noting he had played well enough to make the team, but Brooks would send him back for his senior year as captain at Vermont and maybe call him up just before the Olympics if necessary. Brooks was dumbfounded and said that was exactly his plan.

But there was a chance Brooks might change his mind on a couple of players based on the championship game, so I made one request. After the game, if he was going to make even one change, he could give me a thumbs-down, and I would leave the conditional phrases in place to cover up whatever mistakes there were. But if he decided not to make any changes, he could give me a thumbs-up, and I would notify my desk to pull out all the conditional phrases, meaning we would be the only outlet with exactly the correct Team USA roster. He agreed to do it.

The Great Lakes team trailed Midwest, 2–0, after one period on goals by Neal Broten from Phil Verchota and by Mark Pavelich from John Harrington and Bill Baker. But Homola scored on a breakaway in the last minute of the second period to cut it to 2–1, and big defenseman Ken Morrow scored twice in the third period to boost Great Lakes to a 3–2 lead. Homola scored his second of the game 36 seconds later to clinch a 4–2 victory for Bill Selman's Great Lakes team after goaltender Bruce Horsch had an acrobatic final 10 minutes.

Having submitted my story, I looked over at Brooks. He looked my way, smiled, and gave me a thumbs-up. I quickly called the desk, which did a great job of editing out the conditional qualifying words, and the *Minneapolis Tribune* scooped the world on the team selections.

That tale of intrigue was not to boast, but to make a point. Every game at the Sports Festival was high octane and commanded full attention of Brooks and his advisers, right down to making a final determination at 11 p.m.

The movie *Miracle* did an impressive job of compressing three hours of details into two hours and used Herb Brooks as technical adviser, which kept it pretty accurate on most facts. But at the start of the festival, the Brooks character in the movie tosses a list to the Craig Patrick character and says: "These are the players I want." The Patrick character questions Brooks because the games hadn't started yet. The filmmakers obviously were trying to show how sure of himself and forceful Brooks was, but instead they made him look arrogant and in the process diminished the work done by Brooks, his volunteer advisers, and all the players who went all out playing at the Sports Festival tournament.

Brooks was a complex personality, but his long and studious connection to the sport contributed to his coaching techniques. "I was the last guy cut in 1960, the day before the team played at Squaw Valley," Brooks told me. "I was fortunate to last that long, with guys like Tommy Williams and Billy Christian that were such better players.

"With this thing, I've worked hard to be honest, and I tried to look at it all through the eyes of the players. We can't have all the same type of players; we've got to build a house out of all different kinds of bricks. We can't be all speed. The Europeans all have strength in close quarters, so we can't overlook body strength. I recognize the players' ability, their sacrifices, and I'm trying to complement those with management putting in the same sort of effort. If we remove all politicking, any mistakes will be honest ones. They all have liabilities, but we want to be positive. I want all the advisers to zero in on what the players *can* do, rather than what they *can't* do."

At the end, the official roster showed: Goalies—Jim Craig,

Steve Janaszak, Bruce Horsch; Defense—Bill Baker, Ken Morrow, Jack O'Callahan, Mike Ramsey, Bob Suter, Jack Hughes, Les Auge, and Gary Ross; Forwards—Neal Broten, David Christian, Steve Christoff, Mike Eruzione, John Harrington, Mark Pavelich, Mark Johnson, Rob McClanahan, Buzz Schneider, Dave Silk, Eric Strobel, Phil Verchota, Mark Wells, Ralph Cox, and Dave Delich.

And nobody who was at the Broadmoor National Sports Festival questioned any selections.

4

Endless Herbies

A<small>T THE</small> U<small>NIVERSITY OF</small> M<small>INNESOTA,</small> Brooks was a serious taskmaster, always making sure his teams were in the best possible condition. His most famous practice routine came when he revised what many youth hockey coaches call "lightning drills." In lightning drills, the players line up on the end boards, and on the whistle, they all skate hard in a sprint to the center red line, then do a quick stop and skate hard backward to the near blue line, then sprint again to the far blue line, back to the center line, and then sprint to the far end. Brooks made the players sprint from the end to the near blue and back to the end boards, then to the center line and back to the end boards, then to the far blue line and back to the end boards, and finally all the way to the far end, and back, full length.

Those killer drills, always repeated several times, became universally known as "Herbies" to Gopher players, and the Gophers were virtually unbeatable in the third period because of their great conditioning. Jack Blatherwick, who became Brooks's trusted conditioning expert, convinced Brooks years later that those drills, at the end of a long practice, could be counterproductive to the quickness Brooks was seeking. Brooks said part of the reason for doing them was mental, pushing themselves as an act of discipline when they're tired, and for unity. Blatherwick proved his point by doing experimental work with Minnesota track coach Roy Griak on what type of drills are best for short-burst sprinters, and he borrowed from it to develop a unique conditioning program for the 1980 Olympic team. Brooks carried those ideas through to design quick-interval practices that involved game-condition situations.

But Brooks didn't abandon the Herbies during the training and exhibition time with Team USA, which led to another colorful part of their exhibition tour, and one that was popularized in *Miracle*. This one really did happen.

The 61-game exhibition tour started with two games in Holland, then on to Finland and Norway, for a total of ten games in fifteen nights, concluding with two games in Norway on September 17 and 18, 1979. Those games were important because Brooks could try some line combinations and further his unique playing systems, which emphasized some weaving, puck-control plans on offense, transitioning to rock-solid defense, and using the big international ice. The Olympic games would all be played on international rinks, with their 200-by-100-foot dimensions, compared to the North American 200-by-85-foot size. And the Lake Placid rink is 200 by 100. Finishing with Norway also lightened the road-trip load, because they were not going to be contenders in the Olympics, but they were on Team USA's schedule of Olympic pool play.

What should have been a breeze, however, became something else. Team USA was flat and went through the motions in the first of the two games, and when Norway played hard, the US couldn't click it into a higher gear. The game ended in a 3–3 tie, and Brooks was incensed. After the postgame handshakes and exchanges of good sportsmanship, Brooks blew his whistle and said, tersely, "Over here."

Players from other colleges on the US team wondered what was up, but the former Gophers on the squad knew instantly what was happening. While the last of the departing fans walked toward the exits, they looked back and saw Brooks running his players through an exhausting round of Herbies. He said that since they hadn't used any energy up during the game, he would make sure they used a little up afterward. Down and back they went, and when they finished, he'd say, "Again," and off they'd go, over and over.

Phil Verchota reflected years later that it was nothing new for the Gophers on the team, but it went on and on, for roughly a half hour. The arena staff was anxious to go home, but Brooks kept it up. Finally, somebody shut off the lights in the arena. Still, Brooks kept saying, "Again." In the dark, Mark Johnson crashed into the end boards. When Brooks finally let the players go to the dressing room, he had more than made his point. And it wouldn't be a charade to have Craig Patrick become their ally against this dictatorial coach.

Regardless, the next night, Team USA put forth a full effort and blitzed Norway, 9–0.

As Verchota pointed out, "A lot of the guys thought they had never been pushed so hard in practice, but for those of us who had played for Herbie with the Gophers, everything we did with the Olympic team was nowhere near as tough as we'd already done with the Gophers."

Only 51 exhibition games remained, all on the road, of course, ending when Team USA would meet the powerful Soviet Union in Madison Square Garden on February 9, 1980, on their way to Lake Placid. And already lessons had been engraved.

In its globe-spanning 61-game exhibition tour, Team USA went 42–16–3, which was impressive considering that Brooks was experimenting with different lineups off the 26-man roster, and also trying different line combinations. After returning from Europe, Team USA launched into some NHL games against the Minnesota North Stars, St. Louis, Washington, and then some minor league clubs.

"We played Janaszak in goal against the Washington Caps, Horsch against St. Louis," Brooks explained. "We wanted to go with Craig, but he'd had a pulled groin. That's the American way—No. 1 gets the job, so we're going to Craig in big games. He's the one who can turn a game around. He's got a lot of poise, stands on his feet, good concentration, controls rebounds, knows his angles, and doesn't come unglued. He's solid and he knows his way around the net.

"Craig was our MVP in Moscow. I had followed him and saw him at the Great Lakes Tournament at Christmastime. He wasn't that hot, but he became No. 1 when he got a chance, and played very well when we beat and tied Finland, and tied the Czechs 2–2. At the Sports Festival, he hurt his hand, but I went on his track record. His goals-against so far is 1.5, and he hasn't given up any cheap goals—the kind that can demoralize a team."

Adding and subtracting exhibition games became the norm. The team made a side trip to Flint, Michigan, that Brooks said was a fund-raiser with a clinic for Ken Morrow Day and also because Mark Wells had played with Morrow at Bowling Green. In my reporter's role, I covered the North Stars at home and on the road, and with a game at Buffalo approaching, I contacted Scotty Bowman by phone because he had recently left Montreal to take over as Buffalo coach. He was quick to point out how much he admired Team USA.

"We've got a good team, but we lack speed," Bowman said. "I think next you'll see the NHL get back to skaters, and the big, lumbering guys won't make it. I've been watching the US team, and in Brooks, they've got a top coach. He's good with fundamentals, and he's got those guys flying. I especially like Mike Ramsey. I think they're better trained than the Canadian junior kid we just sent back to his junior team."

It didn't seem that Bowman would have time to go see the US play in so many obscure venues, but he said, "I'm watching them right now—I record their games. They just beat Canada 6–0. Craig was good in goal and Neal Broten got three in the second period, and Christoff, Schneider, and Baker got the others. They're well-skilled and Brooks has done a good job; they'll know what to do. The trouble with the NHL is there has been no improvement, nobody comes up with something different, and they all play the same way. Look at Europe . . ."

Bowman's fixation on Ramsey was because he had drafted Ramsey in the first round as a freshman at Minnesota. "When I want somebody, I don't care where I draft him, just so I get him." Ramsey, of course, went on to play 18 years in the NHL, mostly with Buffalo, and later with Pittsburgh and Detroit before turning to coaching.

With so many former Gophers on the US team, their game against Minnesota on October 23 was interesting. Rob McClanahan said: "It was strange playing against them. I wanted to play well, and it was weird when they played the Rouser and to be on the other side."

Minnesota defenseman Peter Hayek said: "A lot of us had rubber legs in the first period. At times we stayed with them and at times their forwards had a field day."

McClanahan and Mark Johnson scored in the first 4 minutes for a 2–0 US start. Mike Knoke countered for Minnesota, but

McClanahan scored again for a 3–1 first period. Christoff, another ex-Gopher, scored twice in the second period, sandwiching a goal by Minnesota's Steve Ulseth, who was assisted by freshman Aaron Broten and senior Tim Harrer—three players all on Brooks's short list if he needed a replacement. Mark Johnson scored two more goals in the third period, and BU's Dave Silk caught a breakaway pass from Ramsey to complete an 8–2 victory. Johnson, the former Badger villain in games against Minnesota, acknowledged, "I was born in Richfield, but my blood is in Madison."

"Mark Johnson is a helluva player," Brooks said, after that October 23, 1979 game. "He has all the skills, and if he wants to play in the NHL, he will. He's happier for other players when they score than when he scores himself. You despise him when he's on the other team, because he kills you."

Back among the minor-league pros, the US faced some physical battles, which Brooks also wanted. On November 4, Birmingham came to Met Center, and the US showed its tempo, scoring in every period for a 5–2 victory. Christoff scored midway through the first period with both sides a man short, Silk opened the second period with a goal, and Mike Eruzione scored a power-play goal at 19:59 of the second for a 3–1 lead. A Birmingham player took a run at Eric Strobel, and Ramsey—the teenager—flattened the Birmingham player at the crease as Eruzione plunked the rebound for a 3–1 lead. Baker scored a power-play goal late in the third period, and later, Bob Suter fired a shot that glanced in off McClanahan's skate for the 5–2 final. What Brooks liked best was that "Over the last 10 games we've only given up 14 goals—we're not beating ourselves."

On November 20, Salt Lake City paid a return visit to face the US at Met Center, and after McClanahan opened with a goal, Salt Lake City scored three straight against Jim Craig for a 3–1 lead. Doug Palazzari, a pint-sized All-America at Colorado College

who hailed from Eveleth, and would later become director of USA
Hockey, was zooming all over the ice and scored the third Salt Lake
goal. McClanahan's second goal of the game cut it to 3–2 in a second period when the US fired 19 shots on goal, and the US skated
away in the third when Mark Pavelich, McClanahan—for the hat
trick—Mark Johnson and Christoff all scored for a 6–4 victory.

"I got some confidence now," said McClanahan. "If I was still at
center, I'd be on the fourth line, and at left wing I know I can score.
Last year at Minnesota, I was at center with Christoff, who had 39
goals, and Don Micheletti, who had 37, so I didn't have to score. I
could be a two-way center. But I always knew I could score. I got 40
goals my senior year in high school, and I'm learning when to go and
when I don't have to."

On November 27, Canada's Olympic team came to Met Center,
and the thought of that 6–0 loss Scotty Bowman liked so much must
have been on their minds. McClanahan, with the hot hand, scored
a power-play goal with Mark Johnson's pass for a 1–0 first-period
lead, before 6,203 fans. But Canada's Stelio Zupancich tied it early
in the second period, which ended with some heavy hits on both
sides. At 1:39 of the third period, Glenn Anderson pulled the puck
back on a rush up the slot and zinged a 35-footer past Craig for a
2–1 win. Anderson, who went on to a starring role with Wayne
Gretzky's Edmonton Oilers, showed off his NHL shot, as Canada
won despite being outshot 42–27. Bob Dupuis was the unknown
goalie who made 41 saves. "He's the same kid who played against us
up there," said Brooks, meaning the 6–0 US win.

"I'm from North Bay [Ontario] and I've been playing for the
Barrie Flyers in the OHA Senior league," said Dupuis. "I'd like to
think I played a steady game. I'm 27, and I've got a wife and two
kids, so pro hockey is not the big deal it once was to me. I made 41
saves in a shutout against Edmonton, but nobody seems interested.

We've got four guys 27 and older, and we're going for a medal. They played hockey tonight; both sides were chippy up there."

On the last weekend in November, Minnesota went to Grand Forks and was swept by the North Dakota Fighting Sioux, 6–3 and 7–6 in overtime. Gopher winger Tim Harrer scored the first goal of the game and sniped three more in the second period, and Aaron Broten tied it at 0:11 of the third period, before the Fighting Sioux—who later had to give up that wonderful nickname when the PCA (Politically Correct Activists) came calling—won it 7–6 in overtime. Sioux coach Gino Gasparini said: "If Tim Harrer can't play for the US Olympic team, I'll get out of coaching. He's one of the best forwards in college hockey, and he's the best shooter."

One night later, at Met Center, Team USA showed they had hit stride without Harrer's rifle, scoring two goals each period to beat Cincinnati of the Central League 6–1. Schneider and Broten scored in the first period, David Christian and Schneider in the second, and Neal Broten and McClanahan in the third. As if to prove the adage that Brooks's Gopher teams used to hand out on maroon pins with gold writing: "Hockey is for Tough Guys," the US engaged their visitors in some rough exchanges in the second period, including a major scrap with four minutes left, as Jack O'Callahan and Bill Baker took on two or three foes and drew major penalties.

Later that same week, Oklahoma City, the North Stars farm team, came to Met Center and brought some familiar faces. Alex Pirus, from Notre Dame, gave Oke-City a 1–0 lead with assists to US cut Dave Delich and former Gopher captain Bill Butters, before Christoff and Phil Verchota scored in the second, and Christoff, Verchota, and Mark Johnson built the US lead to 5–2 before Jim Boo, another former Gopher, scored in a 5–3 finish. Louie Levasseur made 40 saves in the Oklahoma City nets, to Jim Craig's 25. Levasseur is a wealth of hockey trivia answers. He played one game for the North Stars in the NHL in the 1979–80 season, giving up 7 goals; he played for the Minnesota Fighting Saints in the old World Hockey Association, with 30 games in the 1976–77 season, where he had a 15–11–2 record and a flashy .920 save percentage; and he played parts of two seasons with the Johnstown Jets, a Saints farm team that was the basis for the cult movie sensation "Slap Shot," starring Paul Newman, with the Charlestown Chiefs portraying the Johnstown Jets.

Delich, who said Brooks told him to keep working, said, "I've been trying to keep some of his ideas in mind in the pro system." He seemed to be doing OK, because in nine games since returning from a separated shoulder, Delich had scored 6 goals, 7 assists for 13 points, and for 36 games over the season he had 32–52–84, after scoring 111 goals in 150 games at Colorado College.

One of the USSR's elite teams, Gorky Torpedo, toured the US for several games, including five with Team USA, one of which was at Met Center on December 30. The Russians had beaten the Gophers 8–6 on December 29, but Team USA steamrolled by them 10–3, getting goals from Verchota, Schneider, and Christian in the first period, Silk and McClanahan in the second, and Eruzione, Christoff, Schneider, Christian, and Schneider again, for the hat trick, in the third. The US outshot Gorky Torpedo 47–17. "We had the puck most of the night," Brooks said. "You think they underestimated us? Damn right! We're throwing their stuff right back at 'em. I changed all our lines for tonight."

Badger Bob Johnson brought his Wisconsin Badgers to Met Center to face Team USA on January 15, and the game drew 6,401. The teams were 0–0 after one, but the US took a 3–1 lead in the second when John Harrington, Phil Verchota, and Christoff scored against Theran Welsh's breakaway goal for the Badgers. McClanahan's goal in the second period was matched by Peter

Johnson, Mark Johnson's younger brother and the second son of Coach Johnson. Christoff blasted in a 40-foot short-handed goal and David Christian added another for the 6–2 finish. Wisconsin's Jay MacFarlane caught Mark Johnson and upended him with a big hit late in the second period. Afterward, Mark Johnson said he had a charley horse in his left leg and hurt his left hand badly enough to require X-rays. His dad walked by on his way out of the arena and, while some dads might have said good-bye, Badger Bob said, "Keep your head up."

January finished in what seemed a blur, although Brooks had to lose all his forcefulness to make sure his team carried out its trip to Warroad, Minnesota, to face the Warroad Lakers, the senior men's team where David Christian's dad, Billy Christian, still played. AHAUS officials wanted to scratch the busride, but Brooks insisted, just because he knew and appreciated all that the town of Warroad, Cal Marvin, the Christian family, and the entire culture of the Lake of the Woods borderland meant to hockey, and this was a chance for a small repayment.

Then it was February, and getting near the end of the long exhibition tour.

In Brooks's fertile mind, there were no limits on what can be done on a hockey rink. Lou Vairo was irritated that Brooks got so much credit for copying the Russian hockey style, while Vairo had brought that style to Austin, Minnesota, when he coached a junior team, and it was the first North American team to attempt to copy the Russians. But Brooks wasn't copying the Russians, or anyone else. He took certain elements from a variety of sources, including some tactics from the Russians, to formulate a combination of systems into what he called his "hybrid" style of hockey.

He had chosen players he was confident would be receptive to learning and executing a style with certain rules for defensive coverage, and other loose rules for getting open for passing and play-making. When he saw something that might make his style difficult to execute, he simply improvised and invented a new and better trick to keep advancing. His ultimate objective was to put his players into situations where they might have the best opportunities to create plays and then stressed that they each should depend on their own instincts and abilities to make plays.

His favorite explanation of all his concepts was to call it "sophis-ticated pond hockey." His reasoning was that no matter how strictly disciplined a system was, when practice was over and the players had a chance to engage in a little open hockey, they were having the most fun and were at their most creative.

As Gophers coach, Brooks came to admire those qualities in his recruiting. As a player who grew up on St. Paul's East Side and won a state high school championship at St. Paul Johnson, he was well aware of the rivalry between Twin Cities schools and the Northern Minnesota teams that dominated state hockey in its formative years. And that's why he valued the impact of players such as Mark Pavelich, David Christian, Neal Broten, John Harrington, Buzzy Schneider, and Bill Baker and blended them into the roster. He put an Iron Range Line together with Pavelich, from Eveleth, centering Harrington, from Virginia, and Schneider, from Babbitt; and that line avoided the frequent alterations that shook up other lines and stayed intact as the "Conehead Line," sharing the same instincts and inventing inspirational plays in practically every situation.

What was priceless about that nickname is that I assumed Brooks gave it to them, after the hilarious *Saturday Night Live* tele-vision sketches featuring Dan Aykroyd and Jane Curtin as visitors from space trying to look normal as they fit into US culture. But when I asked Brooks about it, he didn't know anything about the

Coneheads, and said he had never watched *Saturday Night Live*. There probably was a hockey game on a different channel.

The Coneheads themselves were so eager to play that they didn't mind being skipped over for power plays and penalty-killing duties at the start of camp. And when Brooks and Patrick would run power-play practice at one end of the rink and penalty kills at the other, Pavelich, Schneider, and Harrington were assigned to move the practice cones around for the next upcoming drills. So they agreed among themselves to be the Coneheads. Their intuitive puck movement made their regular shifts seem like power plays sometimes, and as the exhibition tour and Olympics themselves evolved, they got more than regular work, remaining consistent while the three other lines often juggled wings with only the centers staying the same. Brooks continued to strive to make the forwards modular, where any of them could fit seamlessly on any line.

"He did a great job with those players," Patrick said years later. "He literally taught them about eight different forechecks to use for different strategies. He might take them out on a field, or into a gym, and walk them through what he had in mind. Depending on the game, or the score, he might change systems, even during games. He could read the other team's systems from the bench, which is a pretty good quality for a coach. I never saw that before.

"Before a game, he'd go to the chalkboard and say, 'OK, guys, we're going to do this three or four times this game.' And after a while, they would anticipate it and could execute anything he said. It was the best coaching job I've ever seen."

Strong words from Patrick, the son of Lynn Patrick and grandson of Lester Patrick, both of whom remain among the NHL's top administrators. Craig Patrick played on back-to-back NCAA champion Denver University teams before spending eight years playing for the California Golden Seals, St. Louis, Kansas City, and

Washington in the NHL and for the Minnesota Fighting Saints in the WHA before retiring. After serving as Brooks's assistant with Team USA, Patrick became the youngest general manager for the New York Rangers in 1981, and his teams reached the Stanley Cup Playoffs every year until he left in 1986. He became general manager of the Pittsburgh Penguins after that, winning Stanley Cups in 1991 and 1992, and went on to become the longest-serving GM in Penguins history. In fact, he even tried to hire Herb Brooks, his old boss and mentor, to coach there, but Brooks only agreed to finish one season before becoming a scout for the organization. He always looked back to what he learned from Brooks with Team USA.

"Before each game, he'd talk tactics to the players, and I listened," added Patrick. "The only thing I could offer were my thoughts about players—I couldn't offer anything about systems. I'd never seen these systems before . . . or since. After 1980, I thought the NHL might try some of our things, but the NHL went the opposite way, really."

To drill his players until they could move instinctively to openings and capitalize on teammates who did the same thing, it took many hours and a lot of repetition of drills. It came easy to a Mark Johnson, Neal Broten, or David Christian, and to say it came easy to Pavelich would be a complete understatement. Pavelich didn't always understand what Brooks was suggesting, but he advised puzzled teammates, with a shrug, to "just go as hard as you can." Easy for Pav to say; his hockey instincts were like the embodiment of everything Herb had in mind.

Whenever there was any day off, the US team had access to Met Center for practice and played several home exhibition games there. The games didn't draw very well, and although I was covering the Minnesota North Stars and the University of Minnesota games, I enjoyed going out to Met Center whenever possible to watch Brooks run US practices. I used to accuse him that his Gophers practices were more entertaining than the games. With Team USA, he started installing a variety of divergent puck-control tactics with repetition into the style, and it went from being awkward, to mechanical, and finally became instinctive.

During one practice, Verchota and Silk were wings on the same line, and after their line took its turn, they went to the bench at Met Center to catch their breath. I was a few rows up in the stands and walked down and asked Verchota something. Verchota looked back and quoted the famous inspirational line used by the Pittsburgh Pirates: "We are fam-ill-lee," he said.

Silk glanced back and added, "but some of us are adopted."

Great line, and I knew I had to use it, but I also knew Brooks might see it as a breach of discipline, so when I wrote that exchange in my *Minneapolis Tribune* story, I wrote, "one player added" for attribution, because I didn't want to give Brooks any reason to demote Silk.

Twenty years later, Brooks was killed in a tragic rollover crash, when he apparently fell asleep driving home from a celebrity golf outing on the Iron Range in his minivan. The hockey world was in shock at the loss of the charismatic star who also had tried his tactics with the New York Rangers, New Jersey Devils, and for one brief season with the North Stars. Most of the 1980 players came to the St. Paul Cathedral and were among the hundreds of hockey dignitaries from all over the country who attended Brooks's funeral.

I renewed acquaintances with all of them, and when I saw Silk, I recalled that incident. He remembered it well. "When you used that quote in the paper, and didn't say I said it, I knew we could trust you," Silk said.

That was gratifying, because players from the Gophers, UMD Bulldogs, and other Western teams knew me well enough to know I would not betray any confidences, but the four players from Boston University still had to overcome the standard East-West distrust. Gaining that trust repaid me many times over once the games started in Lake Placid, where I was able to get exclusive interviews from any and all Team USA players. When Brooks was upset by some in the media, he said they would not be allowed to talk to his players on game days. I knew he had no intention of enforcing such a demand, so I'd go outside and talk to the players after they had showered and changed and were leaving the arena. The *Minneapolis Tribune* stories benefited from a few of those quotes at the time, but most of the rest of their insights have never been printed and will offer fresh, but 40-year-old perspectives in this book.

The players all remember things but in varying degrees of sharpness from so many years ago, and as aging renders our recollections somewhat fuzzy, my carefully saved notes and quotes still stand as the best evidence.

5

Russians at Full Flight

You want superlatives? Of all the spectacular hockey teams the Soviet Union produced before or since, the 1980 Soviet Union Olympic hockey team that would face Team USA in its final exhibition game on February 9 was the most talented team in Russian hockey history. And maybe in all of hockey. This team with "CCCP" on its jerseys was strengthened, even, from the team that whipped the NHL All-Stars, 6–0, on the same Madison Square Garden ice a year earlier.

The youthful Americans had no reason to dispute that theory, certainly not after the exhibition.

The game against that awesome collection of talent, completing the long exhibition season, would be greatly beneficial, Brooks figured. His young team would get an up close and personal look at the team to beat in the Winter Olympic Games starting in three days at Lake Placid, just a few hours north.

The positive takeaways for the US were scarce after the Soviets overran Team USA, 10–3, in a rout that didn't seem that close. The Americans couldn't even blame the officials, because none showed up for the game! Everybody thought somebody else would take care of such a routine requirement, but nobody did. Turns out, it didn't matter. They did a quick panic-search in the crowd and found a 52-year-old salesman from New Jersey who refereed in a New Jersey junior league, and once he dropped the puck, nobody noticed. Maybe it was because the Soviet Union had the puck for virtually the whole game. Obviously psyched to show off a little, the Soviets scored four in the first, two in the second, and four more in the third. They got goals from their newcomers and their veterans, goals that ranged from simple to spectacular, and at even strength, on power plays, and short-handed. Are there any other kinds they might have missed?

The short-handed goal was the one—if you had to pick one—for the time capsule. Alexander Maltsev, who had scored the first goal of the game, made a short-handed rush up the right side as David Christian retreated, figuring he had Maltsev covered. When he got within stick's reach, Maltsev, at full speed, let the puck slide ahead while he did a little Baryshnikov-style hop step and spin, landing just in time to retrieve the puck and score with a world-class backhander.

Brooks seized the chance to entertain the assembled media afterward in the press room. "I knew we were in trouble when they introduced the Russian players and my guys applauded," said Brooks. "Then Maltsev scored that goal, and *I* applauded."

Before the breakup of the Soviet Union, the USSR (Union of Soviet Socialist Republics) had long since become the dominant power in the world of hockey. The breakup allowed various satellite countries to become more prominent on their own, but after some thorough regrouping, and letting its players go play in the NHL, Russia has returned to the prominence for the twenty-first century, with no sign of letting up.

The best of the new-generation Russian teams can't match 1980, however, when there was no question about hockey superiority. The Soviet Elite League had the Red Army, where numerous top young hockey stars were sent to play, and while they wore military uniforms away from the game, their main job was to skate and shoot and win hockey games. There were also other teams, such as Spartak, the Soviet Wings, and Moscow Dynamo. But the Red Army was the nucleus from which the Soviet National team was formed, augmented by outstanding individual players from other teams.

In 1979, less than a decade after the National Hockey League first acknowledged that the Soviet National team could play competitively against the "obviously superior" NHL, the NHL decided that instead of its usual All-Star game, it would select an All-Star team and take on the Russians in a best-of-three series at Madison Square Garden. The first game was a rough showcase of NHL intimidation, which the Soviets handled quite well. With Ken Dryden in goal and Guy Lafleur leading the offense, the NHL All-Stars won, 4–2.

The next game was similar, but the Soviets had adjusted and beat the NHL's stars, 5–4, rallying from a 4–2 deficit in what was a similar game. The names were familiar, with Vladislav Tretiak in goal, outstanding defense, and an offense led by the veteran line of Vladimir Petrov centering Valeri Kharlamov and Boris Mikhailov. The third and deciding game gained the prominence the NHL had hoped for, and NHL coach Scotty Bowman consulted with various hockey experts at the Waldorf Astoria Hotel in Manhattan as he prepared for the pivotal third game. Both sides had made their adjustments, and while Bowman is one of the most creative strategists in North American hockey history, his decision to consult with some of the top NHL minds might have been a mistake. With the whole hockey world watching, the USSR crushed the NHL All-Stars, 6–0. Bowman changed to Gerry Cheevers in goal, and Viktor Tikhonov had switched to Vladimir Myshkin.

For the 1980 Olympics, the same Soviet team made several additions, adding Vladimir Krutov, a 19-year-old fireball forward. Krutov played regularly with Igor Larionov and Sergei Makarov on the "KLM" line, the heir apparent to the top line of Mikhailov-Petrov-Kharlamov. So strong was the Soviet team that Larionov was left off the roster, meaning coach Viktor Tikhonov exercised his dictatorial power by refusing to play perhaps the two best lines in the world on the same team.

Regardless, the 1980 Soviet Olympic team was significantly improved over the team that dominated the NHL All-Stars, 6–0, and then won the 1979 World Championships. After they crushed the US, 10–3, it seemed only a formality before the USSR—having won every Olympic hockey tournament since the US had ambushed them in 1960 at Squaw Valley—would add to the gold-medal tally by winning at Lake Placid.

Krutov, who scored two of the four first-period goals, finished a hat trick in the third period. And Kharlamov, perhaps the slickest stickhandler in the world at that point—a Gretzky-like talent before Gretzky—scored a neat goal for the 4–0 start. Petrov got one late in the second period for a 5–0 bulge. Finally, Mike Eruzione gave the 11,243 silent fans something to cheer about with a US goal. But Mikhailov responded with a power-play goal in the closing seconds of the second period to make it 6–1.

Phil Verchota, who hadn't seen much action in the first two

periods when a couple of injuries reduced the team to three lines, got a chance early in the third and scored for the US, but midway through the final period, Maltsev did his high-speed dance routine for a 7–2 cushion. Makarov converted a pass from Vladimir Golikov through Ken Morrow's legs, and Krutov completed his hat trick before Christoff tipped in a feed from Silk for the third US goal.

The Soviets finished it with a flourish, while outshooting the US, 35–20, as Balderis, known as "the Electric Train" for his speed and stamina, came out of the right corner, fed Valeri Vasiliev at the left point, and got to the net just in time to deflect Vasiliev's perfect return with 3:26 to go. Brooks had pulled starting goaltender Jim Craig halfway through the second period, and Steve Janaszak made some good saves in relief. Nobody at the time realized it would be the last game action Brooks would give his former Gopher standout.

The US, to its credit, tried to pull off a slick play of its own on a power play in the final minutes but instead found one more embarrassment when Verchota and Strobel attempted a high-speed crisscross at center ice—and collided.

The only person in the building who seemed impressed was Tikhonov, the steely former KGB officer who was a stark contrast to the fatherly and much-loved Anatoly Tarasov, the creator of the Soviet style of play. Tikhonov came to power after several other coaches failed to come close to Tarasov's charismatic leadership, but his strict discipline didn't always seem to blend with the level of talent he had.

Tikhonov, meanwhile, was suspicious of the ease with which his team blew by the Americans. "The US team has a very good future," he said through an interpreter, surprising the assembled media with his gracious comment. "We showed what we can do in this particular game; they didn't. The US was holding something in reserve."

Yes, they were. Scoring goals, for example. There was no need for any alibis from the US players, who were certainly impressed from their close-up view of the puck-moving maestros.

"I never saw so many pretty goals," said Ramsey, the 19-year-old defenseman. "One time they came down and made four passes on the rush, and the puck never stopped."

Brooks said, "I knew we'd be nervous, and my mistake was giving them too cautious of a checking plan. We should have been more aggressive. But it was a good lesson. We learned a lot of things. We're not demoralized; sometimes a good kicking is a good thing for quality athletes. We've done a lot of good things—but not against teams of this caliber."

CHAPTER 6

Shorthanded on Defense

IF THE 10–3 SHELLACKING BY the USSR was a blow to Team USA's ego, in retrospect, it wound up having a greater influence on the Russians. The Soviets knew of Sweden and Czechoslovakia and viewed Sweden as their top threat once they reached the medal round, but they had been uncertain about the US. The one-sided exhibition reinforced the US's No. 7 seeding.

Even Tikhonov's astute insight couldn't prevent a blanket of complacency that caused the USSR to coast through some games and find surprising challenges in others. Their main objective was the final game of the tournament's medal round, which they surmised would be against Sweden for the gold.

The US had greater concerns than the exhibition loss. Brooks had to turn in his final 20-man roster by the next day, and he had a few decisions to make. Jack O'Callahan, the defenseman from BU Brooks wanted so badly on the team, and who had been the top scorer and penalty-minute leader among defensemen, had hurt his knee in the Soviet exhibition, and the injury was diagnosed as a partially torn knee ligament. Mark Wells, the fourth-line center from Bowling Green, also suffered a less serious injury. Goalie Jim Craig hadn't been sharp for about a half-dozen games, Brooks said, and thought it might be partly due to an ankle injury that might require a shot of cortisone. But O'Callahan's situation consumed his attention.

During the previous few weeks, Brooks also had been concerned about Mike Eruzione's play, and even though he was a popular captain and had valuable experience from a couple years of minor-league pro hockey, Brooks wondered if he would be able to play at the necessary level or if the team might be better by replacing him with a quicker, stronger skater and better scorer. During a couple of exhibitions, Brooks had summoned high-scoring Gophers wing Tim Harrer to play, and he also knew that Aaron Broten, a year younger than his brother Neal, was tearing up the WCHA as a Gopher freshman and might be worth considering.

Complicating the decision for Brooks was with nine former Gophers already on the team compared to four from Boston University, he didn't want to increase the mix by cutting Eruzione and replacing him with one more Gopher. Then with O'Callahan suddenly questionable to play, cutting Eruzione could leave only two Terriers while increasing the number of Gophers to 10 or 11. Not good for diplomacy. When word circulated among the players, some of them went to Brooks on Eruzione's behalf, and he ultimately decided to stick with him.

The O'Callahan injury was a drama unto itself. The diagnosis of a partially torn medial collateral ligament in his left knee put Brooks in the position of bringing in a recently cut defenseman at full strength or hope that O'Callahan might be able to come back at some time during the Olympic tournament.

A strain, or a sprain, or stretched ligaments can be worked with, but when there's an actual tear, it usually means surgery and a lengthy rehabilitation. A partial tear leaves the decision between surgery or rest. O'Callahan, and the team, didn't have time for either. The first group of doctors who checked him said there was no way he could play in the Olympics. Trainer Gary Smith said, "After talking to the doctors, I told Herbie he wouldn't play for a month, month and a half."

O'Callahan recalled doctors reexamining his knee. "They said there was no way I could play," O'Callahan said, years after the incident. Then Dr. Dick Steadman, an orthopedic surgeon from Vail, Colorado, where ski injuries made him an expert on knees, showed up. "Dr. Steadman asked if I was OK and was poking around and checking. He made me do all this movement, holding my ankle with one hand and my knee with the other to create resistance, then he'd say, 'Kick forward,' or 'Pull back.' He did it over and over. He was working so hard he was sweating, and took off his jacket, and I was sweating, too. The other doctors were all watching, just like it was in medical school.

"Herbie had said if I couldn't play, he still wanted me to go up to Lake Placid. He said he could get me credentials but I couldn't stay in the Olympic Village, and they'd get me a hotel. Then he said he wouldn't have to make the decision for another day before the official 20-man roster had to go in. Dr. Steadman came back in and said, 'I'm going to encourage coach not to take you off the team. Other doctors think you can't play, I think you can.' He said he wanted to come back at 6 p.m. the next day and reexamine me and said if there's a 25 percent chance you can play, we'll do it."

O'Callahan said he spent 40 hours with a trainer, working in precise intervals of stretching, strengthening, resting, and having electrical stimulation in each repeated cycle.

"When Dr. Steadman tested me the next day, Herbie was there," O'Callahan said, "and the other doctors concurred that my healing was so incredible that if I could improve as much for another day or two, I might be able to get back on the ice. Herbie said, 'I'm going to keep you. I don't know how much you're going to play, but I need you on the team. If you're not playing, I need you to support the team.'"

OC's sheer determination was conclusive evidence of why Brooks's instincts about him were accurate. And the relationship was one of mutual respect.

"Herbie had done such a tremendous job coaching that by Lake Placid we had become an extension of his mind," O'Callahan said. "We were so fit, and so conditioned, but we were all worried, too. Even Mark Johnson, who was our best player, was afraid of being cut. At Lake Placid, we finally could quit listening to him, but he had the last laugh, because he already resided in our heads and our hearts. All he had to do was open the door."

The move was doubly risky because while nobody could guess how long it would be for O'Callahan to return to the ice, Bob Suter was still suffering the effects of a broken ankle that had slowed him from regaining full speed as well, leaving the team with only four healthy defensemen. Those four included converted forward David Christian and Mike Ramsey, still only 19 years old. Billy Baker and Ken Morrow were the two solid experienced defensemen. Turns out, there was no need for concern because Ramsey stepped up and became a solid leader with jarring body checks, and Christian was nothing short of spectacular fulfilling Brooks's hopes he would be an effective offensive defenseman.

When asked to recall the pressure of facing some of the best forwards in the world on a unit with only four defensemen, Christian said, "It was awesome. You couldn't ask for anything more."

Christian, who was 20 and had been drafted by the Winnipeg Jets in 1979 while at North Dakota, always was eager for more ice time, so playing every other shift wasn't a problem, but an opportunity. Growing up in Warroad, Minnesota, where his dad, Billy, and uncle, Roger, had built the Christian Brothers hockey stick factory after being standouts on the 1960 gold medal US team, Christian was quick to take advantage of the unlimited ice time for youth hockey players, and he treated every game in Pee Wee, high school, college, Olympics, or NHL with the same intensity.

Nearing the 40th anniversary of the 1980 games, Baker said, "One of the things I'm most proud of is that we won the gold medal basically playing four defensemen. And when Herbie made the decision to keep OC, it showed he planned to go with four, because Bobby Suter was just coming back. And not only was Rammer still 19, but David Christian was one of the best forwards I ever played against, and here he was, my partner, playing fantastic every game at defense."

Ramsey played with Morrow after O'Callahan went out, and as the Games progressed, that tandem was outstanding, as well. O'Callahan remembers being declared ready for the third game, against Norway, but he banged up his knee in his last workout. "Herbie was mad at me for that and didn't let me play until the fourth game, against Romania," O'Callahan said.

Suter was still hampered as he paired with O'Callahan, so Brooks double-shifted Ramsey with O'Callahan when he did get in for spot duty against Romania and West Germany. Suter was another player Brooks wanted for his intense competitiveness. "He was a wild man," O'Callahan recalled, which was interesting because some might have used the same term to describe O'Callahan. As of the 40th anniversary of the 1980 Miracle, Suter was the only player lost from the roster, having died of a heart attack at age 57 while at Capital Arena in Madison on September 9, 2014. After the Olympics, Suter had played some minor-league pro hockey before starting a sporting goods business in Madison and had joined the Minnesota Wild as a scout after his son, Ryan, had been acquired by the Wild and continued a career as one of the best defensemen in the NHL. As a player at the University of Wisconsin, Suter was an antagonist that other teams hated to play against but was much loved by his teammates—qualities both appreciated and sought by Brooks on that 1980 team.

In the upcoming Olympic competition, the goaltending of Craig and the big goals command the spotlight, but the players know that the remarkable defensive play and puck-moving offense of the basically four-man defense was probably the key to Team USA's success.

7

Let the Games Begin . . .

In European hockey, the Soviet Union stood at the top, but great respect was reserved for the impressive rise in skill and success of first Czechoslovakia and then Sweden and Finland. But in North America, everybody admired the Russians because of their frequent trips to play pro and college teams in the US, and nobody knew anything about Sweden and Finland. That might have been a good thing, in sorting through the many pieces of the puzzle for Team USA's "perfect storm."

The 1979 World Championships didn't help the Americans learn more about Sweden, either, because they were in Group A while the US struggled in Group B. Sorting out the Olympic pools off the 1979 results was also not important to Team USA because every country represented a challenge. In seeding the teams, the top three were all from Group A (USSR, Czechoslovakia, and Sweden), while Finland, which won Group B, was No. 4. In the two Olympic pools, No. 1 (USSR) and No. 4 (Finland) were in one pool, and Nos. 2 (Czechoslovakia) and 3 (Sweden) were in the other. By draw, the US would face Sweden in the first game and Czechoslovakia in the second, blissfully unaware that they were, by seed, considered the top two teams in their pool.

In Brooks's world, anything that threatened to disrupt his idealistic plan was worth a little tilting at windmills, and one of those windmills was the Olympic and International Ice Hockey Federation requirement that after each game, each coach will come to the postgame press conference and bring two of his players for comments and interviews by the assembled media. He grumbled about that to me, and while I didn't think it was a big deal, he said that he was in a long process to unify the factions on the team and this could have the opposite effect by singling out individuals.

Just before taking his players to Lake Placid, Brooks got the word that while Canada, Sweden, Finland, Czechoslovakia, West Germany, and the other teams all agreed to follow the rule, the Soviet Union said, "Nyet." They refused to bring players to the postgame. Brooks was enthused. "Good," he said, "now I don't have to, either."

Ready for prime time or not, Team USA hit the Fieldhouse rink adjacent to the Olympic Arena, where the Red Division teams were playing, to take on Sweden, which was wearing its yellow jerseys, and the US wore the dark blue of the visiting team. The arena was not even half full, a result of the game actually being conducted on a full day of games in both pools 24 hours before the actual opening ceremonies were held, plus being in the afternoon as the opener of a doubleheader. The US was outshot, 16–7, in the first period, but they weren't uptight; in fact, they had some good early scoring chances against goaltender Pelle Lindbergh, who was slightly known in the US because he had been a high draft pick of the Philadelphia Flyers. Another unknown Swedish player was Mats Naslund, who would later become an NHL superstar. But if the US had known, there was no room for too much respect.

There were some crisp body checks on both sides—surprising, for the Swedes—but the US was skating well and trading rushes. Midway through the opening period, Lars-Erik Mohlin in the right circle took a pass from Per Lundqvist and relayed the puck out in front to Sture Andersson, who aimed high left and beat US goalie Jim Craig. The 1–0 lead stood through the rest of the first period, but late in the session Rob McClanahan missed a shift on Mark Johnson's wing, and trainer Gary Smith told Brooks he should probably send McClanahan to the dressing room for treatment of a thigh bruise.

The US players all came from diverse backgrounds, and McClanahan came from the wealth-endowed North Oaks, a gated and heavily wooded area of Shoreview, in the Mounds View school district. While Brooks most appreciated the grassroots character of players from tougher areas, McClanahan's great speed and skill lifted him above the silver-spoon category to Brooks. The suspicion that he still harbored questions about McClanahan's toughness resurfaced when the first period ended.

As he passed the training room, he saw McClanahan on the training table, having already taken a whirlpool treatment for a deep thigh bruise and been fitted with a cluster of ice bags. Brooks asked what the problem was and was told it was a deep thigh bruise, and Brooks, often tactless to make a point, said, "Well, it's a long way from your heart."

McClanahan sat bolt upright on the training table, sending the icepacks flying, and went after Brooks, exchanging heated words as he pursued Brooks out of the dressing room and into the corridor. "I chased him out into the hallway," McClanahan recalled, years afterward. "The Swedish team was right next door, and their dressing-room door was open. They had to be wondering what the heck was going on, because there's the US coach and one of his players yelling at each other."

The second period started as McClanahan hustled to put his gear back on, determined to show Brooks what he was made of. Brooks, knowing the injury couldn't be made worse, probably chuckled to himself, knowing once again that he'd made a player mad enough at him to overachieve.

The US continued to trade rushes with Sweden through the second period, but in the last few minutes, the Mark Johnson line, then the Neal Broten line, then Mark Pavelich's Conehead Line, and then the Mark Wells line played four consecutive shifts that seemed to tilt the rink in Team USA's favor. On its next turn, Johnson's line struck. Defenseman Mike Ramsey fed Johnson, who deflected the pass to Dave Silk for the goal at 19:32.

The third period was another high-paced duel of technical rushes, with both Lindbergh and Craig stopping everything. Thomas Eriksson scored on a goalmouth play at 4:45 to regain Sweden's lead at 2–1, but the teams had to kill a penalty apiece as the clock ticked down to its final minute. With 41 seconds left, Brooks pulled Craig with a face-off in the left corner of Sweden's end. He sent out the Conehead Line, with Mark Johnson as the extra skater, and Mike Ramsey and Billy Baker on the points. Ramsey got off a shot from the left point that was blocked by a defender, but he pursued it and fed across to the right point. Baker had no opening and sent it up the right boards, where Pavelich got it.

Seemingly impervious to nerves as the clock ran down, Pavelich put a little move on one Swedish defender and fed the puck out to the slot, where Baker glided from the right point to meet it. "Pav made an unbelievable play," said Baker. "It came to me and it was like in slow motion. I shot, but I still couldn't see where the puck went."

Fortunately, Lindbergh couldn't see it, either. It had zipped in, low and hard, and Baker's goal, with 0:27 showing on the Fieldhouse clock, had given Team USA a 2–2 tie with Sweden. "That's the biggest goal I've ever scored," said Baker, who was buried under a pile of blue jerseys after his tying goal.

Baker refined that comment 40 years after it happened by pointing out he also had scored a big goal when the Gophers beat North Dakota for the NCAA championship in a 4–3 game but added that the magnitude of the goal against Sweden still had to get the edge.

As they were to learn in the next few days, that 2–2 tie was as big an upset as the one in the big Olympic Arena, where Poland upset Finland in a shocker with major overtones the rest of the way. Romania beat West Germany, also, making it three first-day games where the lower seed had surprised the higher seed.

Craig, who played the best he'd played in a month, said, "That early goal got me into the game. You know, I only lost seven games all year, six by one goal."

According to Ramsey, "We were so high-strung we were ready to snap. If we'd ever gotten on top, I think we would have buried them."

Broten, who centered Mike Eruzione and Steve Christoff, said, "They were big. That's the most physical Swedish team I've ever seen."

The players said those things outside the arena after Brooks, as he had planned, addressed the gathered media alone inside the high school auditorium, which was located just across a driveway from the two adjacent arenas and served as the media interview center.

Inside the auditorium, Brooks handled all the questions smoothly. "It was a big point for us, and we got some outstanding goaltending," said Brooks. "That's the best Jimmy Craig has played in a couple weeks. I knew we'd be facing an excellent goalie in Pelle Lindbergh. I wish the Flyers had signed him when they drafted him last year."

Bengt Ohlson, Sweden's coach, said, "It was all right that the game was a tie, but very disappointing to give up a goal in the last minute. You could see the US players were happy, and we were not."

In the Olympic round-robin plan, there were no overtimes, and ties stood, which made that opening 2–2 tie with Sweden grow in importance by the day.

8

US Wins Big

THE OPENING CEREMONIES AT THE Winter Olympics have become a major showbiz attraction, with overdone, multimillion-dollar, made-for-network-TV costumes and performances. It wasn't that way back in 1980, but it was still a classy arrangement—so classy that it seems unfortunate that it was held after a full day of the hockey tournament.

The ceremony was held on Wednesday night, February 13, outdoors at the specially designed area on Mirror Lake, with raised and sloped platforms in front and on the left side, for each nation to place its athletes. They would march in as a nation and walk to the far end, turn left, pass the width of the arena, then turn left again and march back up to the front to their designated location. Once in place, it made for a very attractive scenario, although the bright sun did nothing to ease the bone-chilling cold.

The US Olympic committee chose to outfit all the US athletes to look like cowboys. Not Arizona cowboys, but Montana cowboys, with fleece-lined rawhide jackets and big, impressive cowboy hats. Had they anticipated the harsh, nasty cold that hit upstate New York that week, a sheepskin parka might have been a wiser choice, and maybe earflaps on those cowboy hats. Brooks, it turns out, wasn't much for playing Cowboys and Indians back when he was growing up on St. Paul's East Side, and when he did, he didn't wear a cowboy hat and never owned one, because he didn't like them.

Brooks was unimpressed when the official outfits were issued, and his stubbornness showed again. When Brooks was asked why he wasn't wearing his cowboy hat, he summoned up his best "dog ate my homework" expression and said he had lost it. Nobody asked how anybody could lose a cowboy hat, but they swung into action to find him a new one. The only one they found was about four sizes too big, so some hasty stuffing of paper into the hat was required to get Brooks into full uniform, albeit as something less than a fashion icon.

The whole thing was an artistic success, as each country marched past the cheering crowd, in unique outfits supposed to provide a glimpse into that country's culture. The USSR contingent wore military-looking uniforms with calf-high black boots as they marched up and took their place. Some of the outfits were fantastic and colorful, and the US was properly casual in their new jeans, jackets, and cowboy hats. With the entire US contingent marching together, including speedskater Eric Heiden, the skiers, lugers, and all, it was easy to overlook that Rob McClanahan missed the ceremony to get treatment on his deep thigh bruise. I was there, back in the audience with Jon Roe and Joe Soucheray, my two reporting partners from the *Minneapolis Tribune*, and we were uncomfortably near hyper-thermia in the near-zero weather, partly because I needed to take my glove off to snap photos.

Once all the national contingents were in their places, I noticed something that most of the audience probably missed. The Lake Placid operating committee released about a hundred caged doves from several cages, to represent peace as they presumably flew away. A couple of them didn't fly away. I've observed birds all my life, so I watched closely as all the doves flew up into the sky, flapping hard as if to warm up a little. I noticed that a couple of them seemed stricken by the freezing temperature, and one in particular strug-gled to gain altitude and, failing that, plummeted toward Earth. It fluttered pathetically as it dropped right down amid the assembled Soviet athletes, until it fluttered no more. A white dove of peace had crashed to Earth at the jackboots of the Soviet Union.

Symbolism? Maybe prophetic?

While turning his attention to the Czechoslovakia game the next day, Brooks found another source of annoyance beyond his ill-fitting cowboy hat when he picked up the *New York Daily News* the next morning and found a column by Mike Lupica, who made a career out of boldly writing provocative opinions. It was long before his appearance on the celebrated *Sports Reporters* show on ESPN, and like many other media members, Lupica was irked that Brooks wouldn't bring players to the postgame interviews. He wrote that it was because the coach was on such a runaway ego trip that he wouldn't let any of his players share in the credit. Brooks fumed.

That next night, Thursday, February 14, Team USA faced Czechoslovakia, the top-seeded team in the Blue Division, even if most international observers thought Sweden was better. Brooks didn't seem concerned about the game, despite the great Czech line of brothers Peter, Marian, and Anton Stastny. Maybe it was because the Czechs favored a very predictable "left wing lock" system that designated all their left wings stay at the top of the circles and never join the forecheck, or maybe it was because the struggling US team had tied the Czechs, 2–2, at the 1979 World Championships.

In any case, a crowd of 7,125 nearly filled the 8,100-seat Olympic Arena, but the Czechs jumped ahead, 1–0, when Jaroslav Pouzar shot between defenseman Billy Baker's legs to beat Jim Craig after only 2:23 had elapsed. Brooks called for a trick play two minutes later on a face-off just outside the Czech zone. He moved one defenseman up to line up as a wing for Neal Broten, while Mike Eruzione went over to the bench as if to go off. He stopped and stood near the left boards, by the bench, and when Broten won the face-off, he stepped across the blue line and passed to Eruzione, who, surprisingly, had been unnoticed by the whole Czech team. Eruzione broke in alone and fired from the left circle to beat goaltender Jiri Kralik for a 1–1 tie.

A minute later, the Coneheads put the US ahead, 2–1, when Buzzy Schneider shot, John Harrington missed on the rebound, but center Mark Pavelich knocked it in. The crowd came alive, and many believe that gaining their first lead in two games inspired the US fans to start the chant that has become so constantly overdone ever since —"U-S-A! U-S-A!"

At 12:07 of the first, Craig made one of several good saves on Peter Stastny, but this time Marian Stastny flicked the rebound in over the fallen netminder for a 2–2 deadlock.

Both teams turned to defense in the second period, but Team USA broke through for two more goals and a 4–2 lead. At 4:33, Mark Pavelich eluded a check in the right corner and fed the goalmouth, where Schneider converted. The game got a bit rougher, but the young US players were not going to be knocked around by the more experienced Czechs, and Baker proved it with a big hit on Frantisek Kaberle, knocking him up and over the boards into the Czech bench, head down and skates pointing skyward. The embarrassed Kaberle picked himself up and took a seat on the bench.

Steve Christoff's forecheck got the puck to Mark Johnson, who deked his way past a defenseman coming out of the left corner and scored with a backhander at 15:28, sending Team USA into the third period riding the crest of a 4–2 lead. The Americans stormed Czechoslovakia's net to open the third, with David Christian stick-handling his way in for a shot and Phil Verchota credited with scoring on the rebound at 2:59. "I didn't get it," Verchota protested. "[Mark] Wells got it."

The goal remained Verchota's on the official scoresheet, but the US was coming hard enough that goals became plentiful. One minute later, Harrington picked a Czech outlet pass out of the air and carried it up the left side, behind the net, feeding out front, where Schneider rapped it in. The two goals in the first four minutes of the third period gave the US a sudden 6–2 lead.

Jiri Novak got one back for the Czechs at 5:36 when his hard pass from deep left glanced in off Craig's skate, but midway through the final period, Johnson's pass sent McClanahan speeding into the Czech zone. A defenseman tripped him, but McClanahan kept his focus and scored as he crashed to the ice, bruised thigh and all, and the US bench cleared to mob McClanahan for his big play.

The US finished off the 7–3 victory despite being outshot by the Czechs, 31–27, with a little hostility. Czech defenseman Jan Neliba blasted Johnson with a crosscheck that dropped him to the ice. Surprisingly, the Swedish referee didn't call a penalty, Brooks was enraged, yelling at Neliba about how he was going to rip that Koho away from him and where he was going to shove it. Then

Brooks took on the referee, who gestured to Brooks with a wave of his hand in front of his face, presumably meaning he was obscured from seeing the infraction. Brooks wasn't sure.

"I don't know what that meant in Swedish," Brooks said, "but I gave him a few hand gestures of my own that I think he understood. It was a cheap shot, and Johnson could be out for a while."

While Brooks didn't bring any players to the press conference afterward, I had already established a postgame pattern to catch up to the players outside in the snow as they left the arena after showering and changing. "A little luck and a little hard work," was Pavelich's evaluation, after his line accounted for three goals.

Schneider, who got two of those goals, said, "We just go with what we've got on our line. We weren't nervous; after you've played in the Hipp, nothing can make you nervous."

He was referring to the Eveleth Hippodrome, an old, brick fortress a block down the hill from the main street in downtown Eveleth. The boards, anchored in concrete, are unforgiving—as are the fans. It was Pavelich's home rink, while Conehead linemates Harrington and Schneider had to invade it every year. Brooks, who had been waiting for the slick-passing trio to get rolling, praised them, branching into a little sociology along the way.

"I kept going to the Pavelich line tonight because they were hot. They set the tempo for us tonight, so they became our first line. They're from the Iron Range, and they have a tradition. This kind of performance is expected of them, by their fathers and their uncles. They're the product of a hungry environment, and what they did for us tonight didn't surprise me."

Back outside, the players understood the importance of their performance.

"We didn't say anything to each other, but we haven't been playing well, even in practice," said Harrington, who carried his evaluative mind forward to become a creative coach of men's and later women's college hockey. "We're just three guys who buzz all over, and Pav has got the eye. We're the Conehead Line, and all three of us thought we'd be cut, and now we helped one of the biggest wins the US has ever had."

The captain, Eruzione, added, "Overall it was an excellent game by everybody. I never saw a team come together the way we did tonight. It was the greatest win for the US, I think, since the 1960 Russian game."

Brooks tried to halt the superlatives, declaring, "It was a very important win for US hockey, but you can't overlook a win in '72 when Lefty Curran made 60 saves and the US won the silver. It's not fair to say this is the biggest win since '60, but it gives us something more to look forward to."

Baker observed, "Tonight was the best, as far as coming together as a team. We're getting stronger as we're starting to score."

Craig, who made 28 saves, stated: "We knew they couldn't skate with us after the first five minutes. So we made 'em try to skate with us."

In the press conference, Brooks brought up the *New York Daily News* column that bothered him. He called out Mike Lupica in the auditorium and said, "If you wanted to know why I'm not bringing players in here after games, you could have asked me. And if you think I'm coming here for my ego's sake, from now on you can ask your questions to Craig Patrick, my assistant, because I'm not coming."

He paused on his way off the stage, perhaps not getting the reaction he wanted. "From now on, the press is welcome to talk to players on practice days, but not game days," he said. I knew Brooks had no intention of enforcing that ban, but it would work as only a minor barrier for the majority of the media who didn't know or recognize the quite anonymous US players.

As he left the press conference, I fell into step with Brooks and asked him why he was giving up the world stage. He said I didn't have to worry, that there was a door just outside the barricade in the arena corridor to keep the media from getting to the dressing rooms. "That's the arena manager's office, and I've already worked it out with him to hide out in there," Brooks told me. "I'll meet you in there after every game, and you can ask me anything you want."

Brooks made the same offer to Gregg Wong, who had covered Brooks's Gophers for years, but he was the lone reporter covering the whole Olympics for the *St. Paul Pioneer Press*, and he had to cover all the other events as well and couldn't take advantage of the coach's offer to keep both Twin Cities newspapers informed.

After going 1–0–1 in two major upsets against the two toughest preliminary round foes, it would take something of a breakdown to prevent Team USA from reaching the medal round in their final three preliminary games against Norway, Romania, and West Germany, while Sweden and the Czechs still had to play each other. Let the rest of the world's reporters—who didn't recognize the US players—sit in the auditorium complaining about not getting either Brooks or US players for postgame press briefings; I was prepared to get exclusive interviews with Brooks immediately after each game, then hurry outside and across the driveway to get exclusive player quotes.

9

Clearing a Flat Spot

IF NORWAY PRESENTED A LESS formidable foe on Saturday, February 16, than Sweden or Czechoslovakia, Brooks and the players vividly remembered the long exhibition game in Norway when the US had to rally from behind to gain a 3–3 tie, earning a long, postgame skate.

Brooks had more than Norway on his mind, because the news was that Mark Johnson had suffered a separated shoulder from being cross-checked from behind in the Czech game, a rough outing that also gave big defenseman Ken Morrow a slight shoulder separation from a different cross-check. Both of them played but were restricted by some heavy taping.

As far as tactics go, Norway coach Ronald Pettersson made an attempt at a technical knockout against Team USA. He acknowledged that his team was weaker than the top Olympic teams, so he deployed a cautious plan to hold down opposing goal scoring that, by staying close enough, might raise Norway's stature. If the US required a scare, that was included also.

Right at the start, both sides were serving penalties when Oivind Losamoen shot from the left point and Geir Myhre deflected it past Jim Craig, giving Norway a 1–0 lead at 4:19. The US put on some impressive offensive pressure, but goaltender Jim Marthinsen was solid, stopping all 16 first-period shots. There was no yelling in the dressing room at the first intermission, as Brooks stressed that he was only trying to massage the US to get back into their rhythm instead of trying to do too much individually.

A Norway penalty 25 seconds into the second period aided the US breakthrough when Mike Eruzione jammed in a rebound at 0:41 on the power play. Four minutes later, Rob McClanahan fed Mark Johnson in the slot, who got off a quick shot, taped down shoulder and all, to put the US up, 2–1. Later in the middle period, Dave Silk was checked off the puck, but Mark Pavelich grabbed it in deep on the left and passed it back out to Silk for a goal that made it 3–1 at 13:31.

Through two periods, the 3–1 count wasn't much reward for having a 32–14 advantage in shots on goal, but Team USA kept rolling, and Mark Wells got one at 4:28 of the third period, shooting off Dave Silk's pass and converting his own rebound. At 11:29, Morrow scored with a low, screened shot from the right point, and the US skated off with the 5–1 victory and a 43–22 edge in shots.

"Coming off a big, emotional victory over the Czechs, I was extremely concerned about this game," Brooks told me afterward. "And we were brutal."

The chance to build up their side of the goal-differential battle with Sweden had slipped some more. Sweden beat West Germany, 5–2, leaving the US and Sweden both with 2–0–1 records. If they were to become the two advancing Blue Division teams to the medal round, and remained tied, the top seed would go be the one with the better goal differential. In the Red Division, the USSR was having no trouble, opening with a 16–0 rout of Japan, then thrashing the Netherlands, 17–4, before beating Poland, 8–1. But the Red Division also provided a surprise, when Finland upset Canada, 4–3.

Brooks said he didn't like the goal-differential rule because it inspired teams to pour it on. "I don't think it's in the best interests of sportsmanship for the Russians to score 17 goals against anyone," he said, adding, "I'm not sure we have enough talent to score 17 goals in five games."

The 5–1 loss was a moral victory for Norway. "We try to defend," Pettersson said. "We managed to keep the score down against Czechoslovakia for 26 minutes."

True, the Czechs were frustrated by Norway's style for half the game, then erupted for an 11–0 victory.

The US players were unruffled by it all. Mark Johnson said, "We won, and it's tough. They only forechecked one and dropped the other four back to defend."

According to Silk, "We were mentally flat at the start, but we knew. We weren't frantic."

And Morrow, who chipped in a goal from the right point, laughed about it being less than a rocket. "Mine was a pass," he said. "I just tried to get the puck past the first guy."

The Olympic tournament kept moving through the weekend, and with the US set to face Romania on Monday, I had time to get to some other games, such as Sweden's victory over Norway, 7–1, while the Red Division had a busy slate. Canada bounced back to beat Japan, 6–0.

One of the more captivating games of the entire Olympics was when Finland took on the USSR and almost pulled off a huge upset. The Soviets outshot Finland, 19–5, in the first period, but Jukka Porvari gave the Finns a 1–0 lead with a great move after seizing a free puck. The lopsided shot advantage grew in the second period, and Viacheslav Fetisov tied it right at the end of a power play at 16:01. The third period started, and instead of the Finns caving in, Porvari swiped the puck at center ice and skated in before beating Vladislav Tretiak with a slap shot from the left circle at 2:38 to reclaim the lead at 2–1.

With that, Finland's coaches chose to go to a completely cautious style, trying only to chip the puck out of the defensive zone, or icing the puck and settling for a face-off back in Finland's end. Tradition says trying to sit on a one-goal lead for that length of time is usually the recipe for failure, but Finland was getting closer and closer to pulling it off. But suddenly, cruelly, the ploy blew up, and with five minutes remaining, the USSR scored three goals in a minute and 19 seconds.

Vladimir Krutov, the youngest Soviet player, took a blue line-to-blue line pass and sped around the last two defenders to score at 14:59 for a 2–2 tie. Alexander Maltsev then rifled in a feed from behind the net by Krutov at 16:07 to break the tie, Boris Mikhailov scored 11 seconds later, and the Soviets had escaped their most severe test by far with a 4–2 victory, after outshooting Finland, 48-13. Afterward, I asked Finnish manager Frank Moberg why the team hadn't just kept attacking instead of trying to ice the puck for the last 17 minutes, hoping to win the next face-off.

"Oh, no," Moberg said. "We never could have beaten them. But coming this close will be great for Finnish hockey."

Such a lack of confidence was startling, particularly for a program that had been training and preparing its players every bit as well as—if not better than—the Soviet Union or Sweden. Having the Finns prepared to a peak from which they might have beaten the Soviets made their belief that they had no chance 180 degrees opposite of the Herb Brooks philosophy.

10

All Systems Go

Team USA seemed to be facing a critical point as it went into its next-to-last preliminary round game on Monday, February 18, against Romania. Misfiring a little on offense, the US had been depending on goaltender Jim Craig and a very impressive, though thin, defensive corps. It was time to put everything in place. Team USA did exactly that in the game against Romania, with all four lines and the bolstered defense all contributing to a powerful and balanced attack to prevail, 7–2.

Defenseman Jack O'Callahan returned to not only dress, but get on the ice for some shifts in that game after an impressively swift and efficient response to training and strengthening his partially torn medial collateral knee ligament. Without him, coach Herb

Brooks had been juggling five defensemen, depending for the most part on four—Billy Baker and David Christian on one unit, and Mike Ramsey with Ken Morrow on the second—because Bob Suter had not gotten up to speed recovering from the broken ankle he suffered during exhibition play.

Brooks started the Conehead Line, but all four lines were flying, and the defensemen were jumping up into the attack. The US fired 20 shots in the first period, taking a 2–0 lead at 12:03 on a clinical puck-moving exhibition. Mark Pavelich dropped the puck to John Harrington, who returned it, and Pavelich promptly passed to the goalmouth for a Buzzy Schneider goal. A little less than four minutes later, Eric Strobel pulled a rebound clear and shot it over the fallen Romanian goaltender, Valerian Netedu.

At 9:34 of the second period, Phil Verchota made a great pass right to left in front of the goal, and Mark Wells scored with a high shot. Romania cracked the 3–0 deficit with Doru Tureanu's power-play goal at 13:40 of the middle period, but the Conehead Line connected again with Harrington pulling a face-off draw back between his own legs to Schneider, whose quick shot hit Netedu and carried past him for a 4–1 lead.

The US, which outshot Romania, 51–21, for the game, made it 5–1 when Steve Christoff scored after a neat power-play pass from O'Callahan at 8:14 of the third. Romania's Alexandru Halauca got the second goal past Craig, but Neal Broten walked around a defenseman and scored at 16:12, followed by Rob McClanahan's goal from the slot off Mark Johnson's feed. That made it 7–2, and all four lines had scored.

"Hopefully, the goals will start coming in bunches, now," said Strobel. "I've been fighting the puck, even when I scored. Our lines are all so talented, it doesn't matter who you play with."

John Harrington and Buzzy Schneider were wondering why the

Coneheads played so little in the third period, like the forgotten line after starting, and with Schneider scoring two goals. But Pavelich, their center, didn't question Brooks. "He's right, I wasn't moving," said Pav.

The victory over Romania improved Team USA to a 3–0–1 record with only the West Germany game remaining in pool play, but some details of the match conflict with the excellent 2004 movie *Miracle*. In the film, O'Callahan made a dramatic return from his injured knee in the medal-round game against the Soviet Union. Interesting attempt at rewriting history, but the records show O'Callahan registered an assist against Romania, and he recalled dressing for the Norway game. "I was so anxious to play that before the Norway game I was screwing around and I banged my knee," O'Callahan said. "As I recall it now, Herbie was so mad, he wouldn't play me against Norway."

The other conflict with the movie was the timing of the second-most inspiring pregame message from Brooks to the players. It actually happened before the team hit the ice for the Romania game. Brooks, trying to prevent any letdown after all the work the players had put in, relayed to me in our postgame session that he had stressed to the players the great opportunity of playing in the Olympics, and the "miracle opportunity" of controlling their own destiny.

"Don't blow it," Brooks said, as he headed for the door. "If you do, you'll carry it to your graves." Then he paused and glanced back at his players to add: "To your fucking graves."

In the movie, that little speech was an emotional segment but was inserted into the pregame speech Brooks made just before the final medal-round game against Finland. Some players remembered it before the third period of the Finland game, when the US trailed, 2–1. Others were certain it happened at other times. But in my possession I have the evidence: an old, yellowing issue of the Tuesday, February 19, 1980, *Minneapolis Tribune* sports section in which my US-Romania game story appears—five days before the Finland game—including Brooks saying he had made that comment as a final warning to avoid a letdown against Romania.

The sharpness and balance of the 7–2 US victory over Romania was matched by Sweden, which ripped Norway, 7–1, expanding Sweden's goal-differential edge over the US. Both teams stood 3–0–1, with one preliminary round game to go.

The benefit we had with our rented apartment being directly across the street from the high school and arenas was that I could get to numerous other games when the US wasn't playing. When Team USA played West Germany in its final preliminary game in the Blue Division, there were earlier games that had tremendous bearing on the medal-round participants. The first was between Sweden and Czechoslovakia, and after that, Canada would play the undefeated and untied Soviet Union.

Czechoslovakia was the top seed in the Blue Division, although Sweden was much more impressive at Lake Placid, an opinion verified when Sweden beat the Czechs, 4–2, which knocked the Czechs out of any hope of advancing to the medal round, having lost to both the US and Sweden.

Mats Naslund, who later became an elite NHL star with Montreal, set up goals by Mats Ahlberg and Leif Holmgren in the first period, scored himself for a 3–0 lead in the second, and assisted on Per Lundqvist's goal with three minutes remaining to give Sweden a 4–1 lead. A goal and three assists in a 4–2 victory was an impressive show. The pressure moved up a notch on Team USA to win against West Germany, just to maintain its tie with Sweden in the Blue Division.

I had a postgame interview with Sweden's coach, Bengt Ohlson, who explained that because of a disagreement between the Swedish Elite League and the Swedish Federation, he had only six practices in which to assemble his team and get ready to start the Olympic tournament. By the time Sweden and Czechoslovakia met as the top two Blue Division seeds to conclude the preliminary round, Ohlson wasn't thinking ahead to the medal round.

"We were more excited to win this game," Ohlson said. "At Izvestia [an annual holiday tournament in Moscow], the Czechs beat us, 5–1. We haven't beaten them in three and a half years. We were underdogs in this game. We are heading for a silver; a gold is too much for us. Gold is out of the question because the Russians are the best. It's tough for the Russians to get motivated when they are so superior."

Ohlson also had praise for the US. "If the US does well here, hockey in the US and Canada will change. The US is on the right track now. They crisscross and skate like hell, like we do. This American team wants to play hockey, not bounce into the boards."

Interesting assessment by the third-year Swedish National coach, a teacher in Leksand, Sweden, where he also coached the Elite League team and developed Roland Eriksson and Per-Olov Brasar—two highly skilled players who signed with the Minnesota North Stars among the earliest Swedish players to come to the NHL. His perceptions about the US team playing the Herb Brooks style were spot on, but his prediction that it could convert hockey in Canada and the US was a bit premature.

Canada stubbornly stayed with its traditional up-and-down, dump-and-chase style for most of the next three decades before the input of Canada coach Clare Drake started to have an influence on Canadian hockey development. In the US, with former Canadians sprinkled into the hierarchy, continuing to copy Canada's traditional approach was an easy path, rather than seizing the ideas of its own innovative Olympic coach. That stalled US hockey for more than 20 years, until coaches such as Bob O'Connor and Lou Vairo coaxed USA Hockey from within to move into a more progressive mode. USA Hockey belatedly started its own version of the nationwide "coach the coaches" idea Brooks had created with Blatherwick, and it led to advanced development programs that improved the quality and quantity of US players from every state. By the early 2000s, names started appearing on college and pro lists from more than just Minnesota, New England, and Michigan, winning spots in proliferating junior programs and on into college hockey and the NHL.

Those facts were unimportant 40 years earlier, when the foundation for new-age hockey was germinating in the Lake Placid arenas. Canada's program was not unlike the US's, going with former college and fringe pro prospects against the professionalized European powers. Canada was making its first Olympic appearance since 1968 at the 1980 games, having boycotted two Winter Olympics because Canadian pros were not allowed to play, while European teams, primarily the Russians, continued to hold jobs that consisted of playing hockey.

Canada couldn't have made a better choice as coach than Clare Drake, who was in the midst of coaching the University of Alberta for a 28-year tenure of excellence. He had made progressive strides to assemble a team with several future NHL players such as Glenn Anderson and Randy Gregg and brought them to the Olympics. Except for being upset, 4–3, by surprising Finland, Canada acquitted itself well, but that afternoon, Canada had to take on the mighty Russians in the final Red Division game. As usual, Canada was prepared to uphold its country's national pride.

Jim Nill scored to stake Canada to a 1–0 lead in the first period, but Helmut Balderis tied it two minutes later, and it was 1–1 at the first intermission. Undaunted, Canada stormed out for the second period and struck for two quick goals. Defenseman Randy Gregg scored 19 seconds into the period to regain the lead for Canada, and Brad Pirie boosted Canada to a surprising 3–1 lead at 2:38. With only 13 seconds remaining in the second period, Alexei Kasatonov scored a huge goal for the Russians to cut Canada's lead to 3–2.

The seemingly inevitable USSR offensive explosion happened to open the third period. Goals 12 seconds apart, by Sergei Starikov at 1:53 and Alex Golikov at 2:05, vaulted the Russians into a 4–3 lead. Canada reinvigorated the crowd when Dan D'Alvise scored at 3:05, stealing the puck from Valeri Vasiliev and cruising in to beat Vladislav Tretiak. One minute after the Soviets gained the lead at 4–3, Canada had retied it at 4–4.

The tension was extinguished by a fluke goal, when Russian captain Boris Mikhailov shot from behind the net and the puck glanced in off Canadian goalie Paul Pageau at 8:41. There was no sitting back with a 5–4 lead, and the Russians fired 18 shots in the third period, clinching the 6–4 victory when Alex Golikov scored his second goal of the period on a shot that ricocheted in off Ron Davidson's skate at 16:51.

After the game, Drake met the media. His University of Alberta teams won six Canadian University national championships and 17 Canada West conference titles, and he also helped develop the Canadian National Coaching Certification and Coach Mentorship programs. His tireless efforts gained him entry to the Hockey Hall of Fame in Toronto in 2017, a year before his death at age 89.

Drake was justifiably proud of his team's performance against the USSR and had a comment about Team USA that sent a chill through me, right down to my note-taking hand.

"We played with lots of heart and enthusiasm, but we weren't able to sustain our defensive game," Drake said. Having just talked to Sweden's coach about the futility of trying for the gold medal, I asked Drake if he thought the Russians could be beaten.

"I think it's possible to beat them," Drake said. "I thought Finland should have beaten them the other day, and I thought we were going to do it today. And if I was a betting man, I would bet the US will beat them."

A Canadian predicting such a shocker on Team USA's behalf was electrifying, if not unprecedented. That was still in the future, though, because that Wednesday was still the "preliminary" stage of the tournament, with the US-West Germany game still remaining to take the spotlight. I had watched other games mostly for my own enjoyment, because across the United States, people had started taking note of Team USA's undefeated run at Lake Placid, but they paid no attention to these other magnificent games.

Having already witnessed Sweden beating Czechoslovakia and Canada playing the Soviet Union to a standstill, what more drama could exist? Those afternoon results assured the USSR (5–0) of being the No. 1 seed from the Red Division, and Sweden (4–0–1) clinched one of the two Blue places. Czechoslovakia finished pool play at 3–2 after losing to Sweden but was eliminated from medal competition because win or lose, the US would either end up 4–0–1 or 3–1–1, and for good measure the US had dealt that 7–3 head-to-head thrashing to the Czechs.

Canada had an even more wrenching elimination from the medal round. With the loss to Russia, Canada had duplicated Finland's 3–2 record, and Canada held a clear edge in goal differential. But Finland earned the second Red spot the old-fashioned way—the Finns had beaten Canada, 4–3, early in the tournament, and the first tiebreaker was head-to-head, so Finland was in and Canada was out.

With the focus always on the next game, there was a lot of confusion among the US players, and Brooks as well, about the medal round. Brooks wanted no part of that intrusion on his concentration. "I stayed away from the Sweden-Czech game," Brooks said. But Brooks knew that the Czech loss to Sweden assured Team USA of joining Sweden as the two Blue Division teams in the medal round even before its upcoming game against West Germany, and he also knew the US had to beat West Germany by at least seven goals to win the goal-differential battle for No. 1 Blue seed.

11

Time for a Comeback

JIM CRAIG HAD NOT BEEN at his sharpest throughout the Blue Pool games, but he was sharp when he had to be in the first two games, the tie against Sweden and the 7–3 romp over Czechoslovakia. It was beginning to look like chances were fading that coach Herb Brooks would give Craig a day off and give goaltender Steve Janaszak a chance, unless it was against West Germany. There was little chance he would make such a move once in the medal round.

While Brooks didn't want to alter the focus on the game, he decided to tell the team before the game that if they make the medal round tied with Sweden at 4–0–1, the No. 1 seed out of the Blue Division would be decided on goal differential, since the two had tied 2–2. To overtake Sweden's goal-differential edge meant the

US would have to beat West Germany by seven goals. That was a pretty good challenge, since West Germany had beaten the Brooks-coached US twice in the 1979 World Championships, 6–3 and 5–2. But that was just one of the challenges.

Getting to the press box early was no problem on that day, which I had filled by watching the two earlier games, and I always enjoyed watching warm-ups. This time, it resulted in some pregame drama. The players went through their usual routine, handling the puck and getting both their shots and their goaltenders ready. Suddenly, a hard wrist shot by Mike Eruzione hit Craig up high, and he dropped to the ice at the crease. He appeared to be out, and it took a couple of minutes while he was tended to before he got up.

That was a relief, although I couldn't tell if he'd been hit on the facemask, on the helmet, or maybe in the throat or upper shoulder. In any case, Janaszak went into the goal and kicked out everything he could, trying to shake off 10 days of dust. Janaszak, who hadn't played since relieving Craig when the US was hammered, 10–3, by the Russians in Madison Square Garden, was the highly competitive goaltender who took Brooks's University of Minnesota to the NCAA championship the previous year.

As a close observer, I believed that the US would have been just as successful had Brooks chosen Janaszak as No. 1, or alternated them, and the players were all behind him. Nobody wanted to see him go in this way, but he was ready.

The teams lined up, and Craig was announced as the starter, leaving me slightly surprised. Craig looked a little unsteady, but maybe I was looking too closely. Then, at 1:50, the West Germans attacked, and from outside the blue line, Horst-Peter Kretschmer flung a 65-footer, and Craig didn't move. The unscreened shot went in!

The US dominated play after that, but after killing a penalty to Jack O'Callahan, the US was given two penalties—to lightly penalized Mark Johnson and David Christian—to one for West Germany. The penalties came at 19:41. The Germans won the face-off, and defenseman Udo Kiessling took an open shot from the point, and it, too, went in. The only two West German shots that were threats in the first period both found the net, and Craig seemed to be having trouble seeing the puck.

It was almost the midway point of the second period before Rob McClanahan finished off a neat passing sequence with Christian and Johnson collaborating to set up his backhand, to give new life to the US by halving the deficit. With a minute and a half to go in the middle period, Eric Strobel sped in and had the puck blocked off his stick, but it went right to Neal Broten, who drilled a quick shot from the slot. At 18:31 of the second period, Team USA had drawn even at 2–2.

Clearly, the idea of winning the game by seven goals had long since been replaced by the urge to just win the game, by any score. The US came out flying for the third period, however, and took charge from the drop of the puck. Rob McClanahan rushed up the right side, cut toward the slot, and scored at 1:17 to give the US its first lead of the night, and the fourth line connected at 4:17 when Mark Wells got the puck back to David Christian, who fired a shot that Phil Verchota deflected in, and it was 4–2.

Christian, a quick and clever centerman used to scoring big goals, had not scored a goal from his new defense position, but he was invaluable at doing exactly what Brooks expected, igniting offensive rushes every time he touched the puck. That was never more evident than against West Germany, when he got three assists in the 4–2 victory. That secured the 4–0–1 record so the US could advance to the medal round tied with Sweden, although yielding the first seed from the Blue Division to Sweden on goal differential.

"It was a bad plan to mention that we could be the top seed if we won by seven," Brooks said to me afterward. "If we played our game we might have gotten seven goals. Obviously, we haven't played as well the last three games as in the first two, but we've played five games and we're undefeated. I didn't want to go into the medal round with a loss."

Some of the players figured out the complexities of going into the medal round. But even years later, I heard Mike Eruzione mention in a talk that when the US played the Russians, "it was in the semifinals, we played Finland in the final." But, of course, there were no semifinals and finals, because there was no actual bracket in the Olympics. The plan was to play round-robin in two pools, then the top two from each advance to the medal round but then are paired up Blue 1 vs. Red 2 and Blue 2 against Red 1 on the next-to-last day, with the extended round-robin finishing with Blue 2 vs. Red 2 and the finale, Blue 1 vs. Red 1.

Furthermore, once the top two from both pools advance to the medal round, their records are erased, except for the one game where they played each other. The USSR stood 1–0, Sweden 0–0–1, the US 0–0–1, and Finland 0–1.

"If we knew that everything goes to equal, we might not have felt so uptight," said Mark Johnson, when I caught him outside the arena exit. "We're in good shape, because the Russians are not playing that well, and Finland will be . . . another game."

Brooks was irritated when he learned that Team USA wouldn't be the No. 1 seed and it would go to Sweden on goal differential; he was hoping the US would face the USSR in the final game of the tournament. As it turned out, when it was over, playing the Russians in the next-to-last game instead of the last game might have been a decisive factor in favor of the US.

Outside, I asked Jim Craig about his play, and he snapped, "Don't worry about me facing shots." But I clarified it, that I wondered how the warm-up incident might have bothered him given the 2–0 first-period deficit. "Oh yeah, I got hit in the throat," Craig said. "It stunned me. I almost blacked out. And I let those two in. I blew the first and didn't see the second."

In my private session with Brooks, I asked him about Craig's play, and he told me, "They blew the first one by him, and he was fighting the puck all night. I thought about replacing him, and I talked to him after the first period. He said he was OK."

Then I asked Brooks if he considered starting Janaszak.

"Why would I do that?" Brooks said.

"Well, because Craig got knocked out cold in warm-ups," I told him.

"He *what*?" Brooks said.

Incredibly, Brooks, who had remained in the dressing room during warm-ups, had never been told that his ace goaltender was knocked down, stunned, and rendered shaky by being hit in the throat by a teammate's shot! Just another example of how everything—planned or unplanned—always worked out for Team USA on this incredible journey.

12

TV Schedule Flap

WITH ALL THE PLANNING AND organizing that goes into something as massive as the Winter Olympics, where a dozen different venues all require staffing, scheduling, and execution, it seems likely that somebody will take issue with something. The hockey tournament at Lake Placid was free of such complaints—right up until the night before the medal round.

Plotting the schedule strictly by numbers was quite logical, when you realize the medal round was not a semifinal and final pairing, but completion of an elongated round robin from pool play. Competing for the medals required the two teams from each pool to play the two teams from the other pool, and all records from pool play were discarded, except for the game the two advancing to the medal round played against each other.

So it was engraved in stone that the Red No. 1 team (Russia) would take on the Blue No. 2 (US) in the first game of the medal-round doubleheader, while Red No. 2 (Finland) would face Blue No. 1 (Sweden) in the second game on Friday, February 22, 1980.

Two days later, on the final day of competition, the two No. 2 teams (US and Finland), would play the first game, with the two No. 1 seeds (Soviet Union and Sweden) playing the later game in what was perceived to be the gold medal-deciding, prime-time finale.

Of course, nobody anticipated that Team USA would barge into the picture with a run that captivated the whole country, commanding more interest than any hockey game, before or since. At home, with their television sets set on ABC to concentrate on the US-Russia game, American sports fans were surprised that it was going to be played in the afternoon and were certainly unaware of the scene behind the scenes. ABC television executives pleaded with the organizers to switch the games, so that the US-USSR battle could be shown in prime time in that evening slot already reserved for Olympic coverage.

The big-money involvement of a powerful US television network might dictate some of the scheduling in the twenty-first century, but not in 1980. When nobody could get the Olympic Committee to alter its schedule, the game between the Russians and Americans remained at 5 p.m. Eastern time (4 p.m. in the Midwest, 2 p.m. on the West Coast), and the Sweden-Finland game would remain at 8:30 p.m., Eastern time, in the ABC Olympic coverage segment.

ABC normally might have correctly figured the hockey game would have limited interest nationwide. But in this case, ABC totally underestimated the magnitude of the attraction, so rather than disrupting its regular afternoon schedule, it would videotape the US-Soviet game and replay it at 8:30 p.m. The pockets of intense hockey interest in the United States were properly perturbed, when informed of it, except those close enough to the Canadian border to be able to tune in to Canada's network coverage.

When it comes to the impact of hockey on a nation, Canada is unsurpassed, which became immediately evident. A Canadian television announcer from Montreal, whom I had known for years from my coverage of the North Stars, told me that in Canada, the whole country had adopted Team USA, and his network had tossed aside its afternoon schedule in favor of televising the US-Russia game live, from coast to coast—Nova Scotia to Vancouver Island. With Canada not even playing, Canadian hockey fans would watch the game of the century live, while American fans would have to settle for videotaped broadcast several hours later!

Some people have said the Soviet Union refused to agree to a time change, but the fact remains, a progressive television network would broadcast the game whenever it was played, live and in red-white-and-blue color.

As our second week in Lake Placid drew to a close, there was one other oblique story I was pursuing. I had watched Eric Heiden win one of his five gold medals in speed skating, and I had made a preplanned trip to visit the Olympic Village where the athletes were housed, and which was to be converted into a prison when the Games were over. But I hadn't yet gotten up to the large house where many of the US parents and families were staying.

"They called it 'Hostage House,'" said Jack O'Callahan, with a laugh, 39 years after the 1980 Games. The only time we could arrange for my visit looked like Friday night, February 22nd, so we scheduled it. As it approached, I realized that was the night following the afternoon US-Russia game, but I decided that we could still do it, just a little later, and I realized that compiling collective interviews from the parents would be enhanced by whatever impressions they had of the game.

On Thursday, the eve of the medal-round showdown, it was a good time to round up all the scene setting that had occurred since the Russians had blasted the US by seven goals in Madison Square Garden just two weeks earlier. Herb Brooks had concocted an odd propaganda campaign about the Russian team, and he delivered it in small, subtle comments to any of his players, whenever he had the chance.

The Russians played more bandy than hockey until Anatoly Tarasov started to develop the players and create a unique style of play back in the 1950s. Much is made of the US Gold medal victory at Squaw Valley, California, in 1960, and it was a fantastic achievement when a group of amateurs and collegians came together to beat Canada, the Russians, and Czechoslovakia to win the first and only US Olympic gold medal to that point. The US was led by Minnesotans such as Billy Christian—David Christian's dad—Duluthian Tommy Williams, the incomparable Johnny Mayasich, Bill Cleary, and goaltender Jack McCartan, and the 1960 Games involve a couple of interesting nuggets within Olympic hockey history.

The US had participated in Olympic hockey since the first time it was played as part of the 1920 Olympics, which was part of the summer Olympics, finishing second to Canada, and then at the 1924 "I Olympic Winter Games" in Chamonix, France, taking second to Canada; but they did not participate in the II Olympic Winter Games in St. Moritz, Switzerland, in 1928, when Canada won again. The US returned in 1932 for the III Olympic Winter Games at Lake Placid, finishing second to Canada, and then finished third behind Great Britain and Canada at the IV Olympics in 1936 in Garmisch-Partenkirchen, Germany. After World War II, when the Winter Olympics returned in 1948 at St. Moritz, the

The Olympic Arena in Lake Placid, renamed in 2005 for 1980 Team USA Coach Herb Brooks, was also the site of the 25th team anniversary gathering. *(Doug Kerr from now in Binghamton, NY [CC BY-SA 2.0 (https://creativecommons.org/licenses/by-sa/2.0)], via Wikimedia Commons)*

Spacious interior view of 100-foot Olympic ice width inside Herb Brooks Olympic Arena. *(Aaron danielg at English Wikipedia [Public domain], via Wikimedia Commons)*

Mike Ramsey of the US checked a player from West Germany during the Olympics on February 20, 1980. *(Photo by: Steve Powell/Getty Images)*

USA celebrated its victory over Russia in the "Miracle on Ice" game on February 22, 1980. *(Photo by: Steve Powell/Getty Images)*

Team USA's Billy Baker (left), Buzzy Schneider (on knees), and Dave Christian (23) helped Jim Craig defend against the USSR. *(Photo by: Steve Powell/Getty Images)*

US players congratulated Buzzy Schneider (25), who had just scored against Vladislav Tretiak for a 1–1 tie in the first period. *(Photo by John Gilbert)*

The US and Soviet Union teams shook hands after USA's 4–3 victory. *(Photo by: Steve Powell/Getty Images)*

An arena view during the US/Finland gold-medal matchup. *(Photo by: Steve Powell/ Getty Images)*

Faceoff during the US's gold-medal victory against Finland. Finland's Jari Kurri (17), age 19, would soon become an NHL superstar at right wing with Wayne Gretzky in Edmonton. *(Photo by: Steve Powell/Getty Images)*

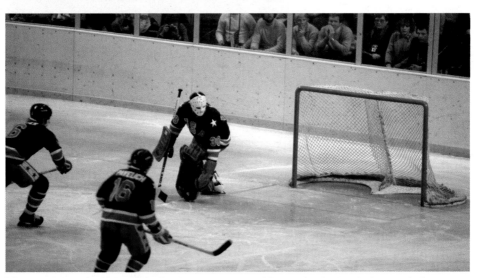

Team USA goaltender Jim Craig watched the flight of a Finland shot as defenseman Bill Baker and backchecking center Mark Pavelich arrived to help. *(Steve Powell/ Getty Images)*

Steve Christoff set up Mark Johnson's short-handed goal that clinched the 4–2 final-game victory and Team USA's gold medal. *(Photo by: Getty Images)*

The US celebrated after its gold-medal victory over Finland. *(Photo by Steve Powell/ Getty Images)*

US players arrived to mob Mark Johnson, whose short-handed goal finished a 3-goal third-period rally to beat Finland, 4–2, and clinch the gold medal, at 6–0–1. *(Photo by John Gilbert)*

David Christian's No. 23 Team USA jersey from the 1980 Winter Olympics hangs on display at the Hockey Hall of Fame. *(mahfrot on Flickr [CC BY 2.0 (https://creative-commons.org/licenses/by/2.0)], via Wikimedia Commons)*

Game-worn jersey at Lake Placid, complete with a few stains of some sort. *(Photo by John Gilbert)*

Medallion designed by Marcel Jovine commemorating the Winter Olympics in Lake Placid, New York, 1980. *(Photo by FPG/Getty Images)*

US took fourth, behind Canada, Czechoslovakia, and Switzerland in the V Games, and the US finished second to Canada in the VI Olympic Winter Games in 1952 in Oslo, Norway.

One thing notable about all those Winter Olympic results is that nowhere to be found is an entry from the Soviet Union. Through those first six Winter Olympic hockey tournaments, the Russians did not send a team. Tarasov finally deemed them ready in 1956, and the Soviet Union entered their first Olympic hockey tournament, the VII Olympic Winter Games, in Cortina d'Ampezzo, Italy, and won its first gold medal on its first attempt, while the US took second, and Canada third.

The US pulled off its huge upset over the Soviet Union and claimed the 1960 gold medal, but amid the warm accolades of that achievement in Squaw Valley, California, it is rarely noted that 1960 was only the second time the Russians participated in Olympic hockey, while it was the eighth time for the US.

The Russians had proven to be the best in the world just in time for their first gold medal, and after losing in 1960, the Soviet Union spent the 20 years from 1960 to 1980 completely dominating the hockey world, winning Olympic gold in 1964, 1968, 1972, and 1976, and all but one World Championship during that same time span—a tribute to its first wave of outstanding players. Vladislav Tretiak was, and still is, considered the best goaltender ever to play the game, and a group of flawless defensemen helped make the Russians nearly impenetrable, but the thing that truly set the Russians apart was their circling, swirling offense.

There had been individuals, such as Alexander Yakushev, who stood out, but from the mid-1960s on, an incomparable first line of Vladimir Petrov centering Valeri Kharlamov on the left and Boris Mikhailov, the captain, on the right was too good to be contained for over a decade.

Aging but not showing their age, each member of that superb line scored a goal in the 10–3 exhibition rout in Madison Square Garden. Brooks, impressed as he was with the Russian style, had always schemed to get his team far enough into the tournament where they might have to face the Soviet Union, and then they could take their best shot. So he started in shortly after that exhibition blowout with a campaign to raise the hint of doubt among his young players. "Did you guys notice Mikhailov?" Brooks would say. "He looks exactly like Stan Laurel."

Laurel and Hardy was a legendary comedy duo from the 1920s to the 1940s, remaining a big attraction in black and white on television and historic shows, too. Stan Laurel was the slim one, almost always puzzled and usually the innocent foil of his conniving partner, Oliver Hardy. Brooks noticed the distinct facial resemblance between Mikhailov and Stan Laurel, and he brought it up repeatedly, always generating a chuckle. Just a small part of Brooks's subtle point that this Russian team may not be unbeatable, after all.

He would add some observations he noticed about how uninspired the Russians looked in some games, how overconfident they must be. "I don't know what's wrong with the Russians," he'd say. "They haven't had their usual intensity . . . maybe they consider this a comedown after having beaten the NHL's best pros. But if Russia takes us lightly, if they play like they did against Finland and Canada, they could be in trouble."

Pushing his players to the maximum physically, he also wanted to toss in a psychological chip by chiseling into the aura of invincibility about the Russians. It was a mental thing to make his players feel better about their chances and their "sophisticated pond hockey."

"When the smoke clears," Brooks added, "I want our players to know that their maximum ability has been spent on the ice."

He drew one final parallel between himself and Russian coach Viktor Tikhonov. "If Tikhonov loses, he goes to Siberia," Brooks said. "If we lose, I go to East St. Paul. That's not bad, because that's where I'm going anyway."

It wasn't long, of course, before Brooks turned to the high-tech tactical game plan for his team against the Russians. "The 10–3 loss in New York does us good, now," he said. "I made the team play a cautious forechecking style in that 10–3 game. Now we're going to try what we did against the Czechs. We'll forecheck aggressively from the top of the circles in, but once they get out past the top of the circles, we'll fall back to set up almost a 1-4 zone between the top of the circles in their end and our blue line."

That was an interesting plan, to combine aggressive forechecking, which could surprise the Soviet Union defensemen, while still paying full respect to contain the explosive Russian offense. The loss in the exhibition paid a few dividends to the US, and Brooks knew the Russians gained nothing from the US play in that game.

13

Game of the Century

As the 1980 Olympics progressed, and the US hockey team continued to win, well-intentioned outsiders continually sought to link Team USA for inspiration, in the face of the major political problems of the world, such as the US hostage crisis in Iran and the heightened Cold War with the Soviet Union invading Afghanistan. But during those two-plus weeks at Lake Placid, the US players were so consumed with their own "cold war" project, it was like they were locked into a cocoon, insulated from the outside world.

"We really weren't aware of the rest of the world," said Billy Baker, thinking back to those days after 40 years had passed. Baker followed up a brief try at NHL hockey by returning to dental school to become an oral surgeon specializing in maxillofacial surgery and part owner of a thriving oral surgery business based in Brainerd, Minnesota. He and his wife, Diane, raised three kids and have devoted much of their time since he retired in 2016 to their grandchildren.

"My parents were at Lake Placid, but for us as players, we weren't watching TV news or reading newspapers. We were so focused on our team, playing one day and practicing the next, that it just was a blur it went by so fast. We had no idea it would become as big as it did. When we had some free time, we'd go to other events. I saw Eric Heiden win three of his five gold medals in speed skating."

To the amazement of the US players, who opened the Olympics with a half-full arena for their opening 2–2 tie with Sweden, the support of sports fans all across the country expanded with each step of Team USA's improbable run. The changeover in little Lake Placid saw Olympic Arena become the site of a cheering, flag-waving crowd that introduced and made popular the "U-S-A!, U-S-A!" chant, and available seats became more and more scarce. It was the same in the press box, which wasn't even half full for the opening game but was filled to capacity with journalists eager to catch a glimpse of the climax of this magical ride that was now running up against the mighty Soviet Union.

My press box seat was the same, and the same man was sitting next to me. His name was Andreas Wyden, and he was from Switzerland, where he was both a journalist and managed the Lugano team from the Swiss elite league. We shared stories and insights into all the teams throughout the tournament, and his insights into the Soviet Union lifestyle can elicit a chill 40 years later.

Inside the arena, Brooks had a few reminders he wanted to go over with his team before the biggest game of their lives, but as soon as he walked into the US dressing room, he immediately sensed from the silence that the players were uptight, which was understandable.

It's possible Brooks even allowed a flashback to 1974, his second year as coach of the University of Minnesota, when he met his players for a final meeting before they faced Michigan Tech in the NCAA championship game in Boston Garden. Brooks had a couple pages of notes as he walked in, and he prefaced it with, "Well, this will be the last time you'll have to listen to my pregame speech." With that, the players erupted in cheering and applause that startled Brooks and sent him laughing out into the hallway. He never delivered the pep talk because he sensed that the tension had been broken, and they went out and beat Tech for the Gophers' first NCAA title.

Maybe the recollection had come to mind, maybe not, but this time, Brooks prepared for brevity, and he delivered what is quite possibly the best pregame speech in sports history:

"You were born to be a player. You were meant to be here. This moment is yours!"

Perfect. The tension vanished, and the players' spirits went right up to the ceiling. Mark Johnson, the first-line center and leading scorer, said, "Herb's pregame speech captured the moment. That's why he was so successful. He had vision, he was the ultimate salesman, he sold us on what he was teaching, and we believed it."

Winger Eric Strobel, years later, stated, "He was a really, really good coach, and as great as he was with X's and O's, his mental approach was amazing. He knew you can't coach spontaneity and that emotion has to come from within. . . . He wanted to get us to the point where we could find our own way, and he knew that sometimes he had to be a hard-ass to get us all to that point."

The US players hit the ice, absorbing the crowd's added enthusiasm, and immediately went to work. The Conehead Line had a good shift with a threat or two, and it was apparent this would be a battle. Brooks didn't hesitate to juggle his modular players, shifting Dave Silk up with Mark Johnson and Rob McClanahan a few minutes in, and shifting Steve Christoff to the Mark Wells-Phil Verchota unit.

At our private postgame meeting, Brooks told me he was worried about how the Russians were pinning his team in its own end with their strategic start. The Russians were sending their strong-side defenseman pinching in from the point to accost the US wing trying to play the puck on the boards. Brooks immediately wanted to switch tactics to an unusual ploy they had tried against Canada in an exhibition. For added support, Brooks asked Craig Patrick to call upstairs on the walkie-talkie to apprise Lou Vairo, his consultant who was a student of Russian tactics, of his plan.

"We started flying the strong-side winger up the boards and out of the zone, with our center cutting across behind him, and we had the weak-side winger drop back all the way to the corner," Brooks explained. "That meant they couldn't pinch in, with the threat of a long pass to our breaking winger, and if we reversed the puck around the end boards to the other corner, our guy was back deep enough that their weak-side defenseman couldn't get to him. We switched at about the eight-minute mark, and we immediately started coming out of our end easily. In a way, we were giving the Russians a little dose of their own medicine, and they didn't expect it."

Being forced to adjust to an opponent's change in strategy was also something that wasn't normal for the Russians, who were accustomed to being adjusted to, not doing the adjusting. Nevertheless, the Russians struck first, when Vladimir Krutov, signaling a new wave of Soviet stars, tipped a point shot by Aleksei Kasatanov past Jim Craig at 9:12 for a 1–0 lead.

Getting out of the zone meant generating more rushes than just defending, though, and that paid off about five minutes later when Pavelich rushed across the Soviet blue line on what looked like a nonthreat, with three Soviet defenders dropping back. But Pavelich had the innate ability to lure opponents to move the way he wanted them to and enhance a scoring chance, and he made a slight veer to his right and sent a pass back to his left, toward Buzzy Schneider. The speedy winger was coming hard, and he gathered the pass in and cut loose with a quick snap shot from 45 feet out in the left face-off circle. It may have surprised goaltender Vladislav Tretiak, and it beat the star netminder to tie the game, 1–1. Brooks was still trying to get all his gunners untracked, so he kept juggling, with Christoff moving to Neal Broten's line, with Mike Eruzione on the other wing, and Wells centering Verchota and Strobel. The Conehead Line, with Pavelich centering Schneider and John Harrington, was the only line staying intact, because all of them spoke "Range" with their hockey sense.

The chances were pretty even, but the red-clad Soviets took a 2–1 lead when Alex Golikov passed to the slot from the right corner and Sergei Makarov sent a quick shot past Craig. That seemed like a pivotal goal with 2:26 left, even though it was still only the first period. The period ended, or didn't end, with an incredible final second that included the play of the game, and perhaps of the entire tournament.

The clock was ticking down when David Christian choreographed the goal that stunned the Russians and changed the course of the game. Christian joked about how so many game details are vague in the minds of all the players 40 years after they happened, but he remembers exactly what happened on this one.

"I was in deep, almost at the top of the Russian crease," Christian recalled. "They cleared the puck, and we skated back out of their zone. My partner on defense was Kenny Morrow, and he had the puck, so I circled behind him. Kenny dropped the puck to me, and as I'm coming up, I realized there were only a few seconds left, so I decided that by throwing it on their net, the period would end and we'd only be down one goal, which wouldn't have been bad.

"I was about at the center red line, and I shot sort of a half slap shot. Tretiak blocked it but then relaxed, knowing time was about up. But there was Mark Johnson skating in, splitting the defense, and getting to the puck. He had just enough time and he made a little deke and slid the puck into their net. The clock showed 0:00, but the red light came on. When the time is completely out, the green light comes on and you can't turn on the red light."

Tikhonov immediately ordered his players to the dressing room, hoping the officials would decide the period had ended. But the officials called it a goal and ordered the Russians to come back on the ice for a face-off that was necessary before the period could technically end. Reluctantly, Tikhonov sent only five skaters back from the dressing room for the face-off, with backup goaltender Vladimir Myshkin in the nets. They dropped the puck and the horn sounded, and the US dressing room came alive with the score 2–2 on Johnson's brilliant goal.

When the second period began, Myshkin was the goaltender, and not Tretiak, causing Brooks to notify his players: "Gentlemen, the greatest goaltender in the world is now on the bench."

They perked up even more from that. "It was a real lift for our team," said Christian. "And it confirmed what Herbie had been telling us, that something was missing on their team."

Years later, after the Cold War had melted, I spotted Tretiak arriving at the Minneapolis airport as I was heading for a plane. He came to Minnesota to work at a goaltender's clinic, and I stopped him and introduced myself and told him I had covered the Lake Placid Olympics, and that another journalist had suggested Tretiak had pulled himself from that game in frustration. I told him I didn't believe it for a second and wondered what he thought of Tikhonov's decision.

"Tikhonov," he said, "was a fool."

Pretty straightforward. More subtle was Boris Mikhailov, the captain, who said on a social media statement that he didn't like to remember the 1980 game, adding, "There were terrible coaches' mistakes in the game. I think there was no need to change Tretiak." However, it should be noted that it was Myshkin who shut out the NHL All-Stars 6–0, one year earlier.

The second period started, and Harrington was called for holding at 0:58, setting up a Russian power play. Alexander Maltsev batted Vladimir Krutov's pass ahead and was in, with a burst of speed, scoring with a shot from the left side at 2:18, a power-play goal for a 3–2 lead. That started a strange period, with the US skating well and getting chances but misfiring or shooting wide. The Russians were flowing on the attack, and Craig's goaltending and the US team defense had its hands full, weathering it, although the US defensemen, young as they were, played with amazing poise.

By tradition, Soviet national teams were routinely outshot but used slick passing to create open chances, leading to key goals when they needed them. Now, with something of a role reversal, the Russian players remained calm, as if still certain that things would work out. A key part of the game was that Craig was at his best, despite one misplay when he went behind the US goal and covered the puck, illegally, and was called for delay of game midway through the second period. It seemed to fire up Craig against the Soviet power play, and Mark Johnson, the top scorer, did a fantastic job on the penalty kill, setting up Buzzy Schneider on a short-handed 2-on-1 chance that sailed just wide.

The Soviet Union outshot the US, 12–2, in the second period, and 30–10 through two periods, but Brooks told his players that they had just as many good scoring chances, and to stick with the system. In the third period, it paid off. Krutov was penalized for high-sticking at 6:47, and on the US power play, defenseman Billy Baker moved in from the left point and passed ahead for Mark Johnson skating toward the right edge of the net. The pass was blocked, and it dropped between the skates of a Russian defenseman. The ever-alert Johnson never hesitated, swatting at the puck and slamming it from between the defenseman's skates into the net at 8:39. The goal did more than tie the game, 3–3; it eliminated the supposition that the USSR winning the game was inevitable.

The crowd was going berserk by then, chanting "U-S-A!, U-S-A!" while standing and waving flags. One shift later, the Conehead Line came back out and almost immediately went on the attack. If this was turning into pond hockey, a rink-rat game on an Iron Range lake, these were the right guys in the right place. Schneider, who never challenged or questioned Brooks, was the picture of discipline as he carried across the center red line and flung the puck hard into the Soviet end, then skated to the bench. He may not have been too tired, but it was a chance to make a change on the fly without any defensive risk, and an early change was far better than a late one. Schneider's linemates were already chasing the puck deep into the Soviet Union zone. John Harrington tipped it behind the net and around the boards through the left corner, where Mark Pavelich was arriving.

When Schneider went off, Mike Eruzione came on as his left-wing replacement, changing on the fly. Billy Baker, the left defenseman, realized immediately that Schneider had gone off, and the third attacking forward wasn't there, for the moment, so he moved in all the way to the crease to attack. Eruzione, if he'd spent the last four years having the Brooks discipline instilled at Minnesota, might have known better and stopped at the left point to cover for Baker, but instead he arrived just late enough to be right on time, skating right on toward the slot.

The mercurial Pavelich got to the puck, under pressure, and lost his balance. His incredible hockey sense made him realize that Baker was in deep, but covered, so he flicked a backhand pass out of the left corner as he fell to the ice. The pass was headed for David Christian at the right point, but as it slid, Eruzione picked it off as he skated left to right to the slot, then he shot, low and to the left. As the whole hockey world knows, his shot found its way through a maze of players that was screening Myshkin and found the net. The red light came on at exactly 10:00 of the third period, and Team USA had a 4–3 lead.

"Buzzy came off early," Eruzione said afterward. "My pal. He owed me one. I kept walking in, and a defenseman screened the goalie, so I shot."

The 10 minutes remaining was ample time for the Russians to rise up and steal another victory, as they had done in the closing minutes against both Finland and Canada. But the US players, who might have thought Brooks was crazy for some of the long practices and constant pushing through the exhibition season—and for telling them to stay with the system when they fell behind earlier in this game—were dedicated to doing exactly what they had prepared to do.

As an aside to that moment, players years later reflected on the preparation, and winger Phil Verchota, who was playing his fifth straight year under Brooks, refuted the notion that Brooks orchestrated every adjustment the team made and revealed the inner workings of the Brooks strategy, to get the players to use their own intuition for instantaneous decisions, and their own skill to execute them.

"I can't tell you that Herbie ever adjusted during the games," Verchota said. "We had one forecheck, and we would read keys to adjust, depending on what the first forechecker did, to whether we would hit, or chase, or fall back. The second forechecker was always keying off the first guy going in. Once we learned it, we never adjusted because we were adjusting all the time. It's just like in business, where you can't teach your employees what to do in every situation, but you can teach them how to think, and they can learn how to make the best decisions."

Setting up and scoring goals is the flashy part of hockey, but in the last 10 minutes of the biggest hockey game in US history, the ability to think under intense defensive pressure was more important than any highlight-video scoring play. The US played with cool precision, despite the crowd screaming every time one of them cleared the zone or touched the puck. Jim Craig made the saves, the US defense cleared the area of rebounds, and whoever got the puck next chipped it up the boards and out of the zone or hit a teammate with a pass. More cheers.

The role reversal seemed to bewilder the Russian players, who became hesitant. The US was not falling back into a shell, but making bold plays. Steve Christoff flattened Sergei Starikov along the boards with a body check, and Mike Ramsey flattened Valeri Kharlamov with a hard check and seemed to flatten somebody else in red on every shift. The Conehead Line had a good shift. Billy Baker swiped the puck from a Russian forechecker and cleared the zone. The instinctive, automatic precision of the Russian skaters now seemed disorganized, and passes went to nobody. It seemed as though the clock weren't moving fast enough, though, before it got down to the last two minutes—which seemed to take a half hour! With 1:55 remaining, the crowd rose in a standing ovation. The US played on. With 1:29 left, a missed Russian pass went the length of the rink for an icing, something the Russians never did.

Andreas Wyden, the fellow from Switzerland sitting next to me, started talking in his low, heavy accent, where only I could hear it. "Look at the Russian players," he said. "Nobody takes the lead, because nobody thinks. It's a reflection of their system. They usually look so calm, so poised, and 'tack-tack-tack' they score. But when they need to do something different, they need to have a practice before they can do it. When the US was behind, they had to invent something, and they did, now the Russians are in trouble and they are poised. But they don't need poise. They need emotion."

The tension had already reached electrifying levels in the arena and in the press box, where the American journalists were unabashedly standing and cheering. I was proud of the fact that I internalized it all, and instead of cheering, I had to keep reminding myself to exhale. Amid the roaring scenario of the moment and the big crowd, here I had this calm soliloquy being delivered next to me, causing my hair to stand on end. I hoped he'd stop talking and not jinx anything, but everything Wyden said was awe-inspiring. And he was right on: the Russian players remained calm and poised, even when they would have been better served by a dose of urgency.

With 1:12 remaining, the Russians went offside—something else that was extremely rare for them in normal situations. The Russians attacked again, and Mikhailov—Stan Laurel in a CCCP-lettered jersey—took a shot but missed the net with 45 seconds to go, as he tried to avoid a check from Mark Johnson and enter the US zone. Still on the attack, Vladimir Petrov got the puck and shot, wide, and 25 seconds remained. The puck was behind the net, and Brooks had the Johnson line with Silk and McClanahan out there, with giant Ken Morrow and teenager Mike Ramsey on defense.

Morrow was checked off the puck behind the net by a Russian fore-checker, but Johnson gained control and slid the puck along the end boards to Ramsey, moving toward the right corner. He ran into a forechecker and protected the puck, while McClanahan raced back to gain possession and nudge the puck back to Johnson.

The Russians never pulled their goaltender, maybe because they so rarely had needed to and hadn't practiced it. Under pressure, Johnson saw an opening beyond the five Russian attackers, and he sent the puck ringing around the left corner boards and up toward center ice, where Silk deflected it past the point man and out of the zone. McClanahan, who somehow had gotten all the way out to meet it, saw he was clear of any Russian skater, so instead of tak-ing possession, he skated a couple of strides alongside the puck as though escorting it out of the final danger.

In those final seconds, ABC broadcaster Al Michaels issued what became his signature comment: "Do you believe in miracles? YES!"

The clock hit zero, the horn sounded, and McClanahan leaped into the air, as sticks and gloves flew toward the rafters and the US players came pouring off the bench. On the bench, Jack O'Callahan was the last to leave. He had been restricted to two or three brief shifts in the game by Brooks, who realized in part-time duty in the previous two games that OC's recovering left knee might not be able to keep up the intense pace. O'Callahan was so involved it was like he was coaching the team, Brooks said later. At the finish, Brooks walked down the bench toward O'Callahan, whose first reaction was to throw a forearm that caught Brooks in the chest and almost knocked him down, "because he was so excited we won," Brooks said afterward, then added, "At least, I think it was because he was so excited."

With the crowd lost in ecstasy, jumping up and down cheering, laughing, crying, out on the ice, the players were piling on top of one another as Brooks turned and disappeared down the runway from the bench toward the dressing room. Four players staged a mass hug on the ice—the Boston University gang of Craig, O'Callahan, Silk, and Eruzione. Craig said, "Just like BU," but after a moment he whirled away from the pack and skated toward the plexiglass. As he gazed up into the crowd, a fan threw him an American flag. Craig caught it, unfolded it, and wrapped it around his shoulders in what would become the symbolic patriotic shawl of all time, and he kept looking up, until he locked eyes with his father. His mother had recently died, and Craig wanted to share his special moment with his dad.

The spontaneity of that moment, Craig wrapped in an American flag, locking eyes with his dad, was so special that it has inspired dozens of participants on following championship teams to try to copy it. Some even stashed a flag with a trainer or equipment person so they could copy Craig's pose, unaware that the extraordinary impact of Craig's pose was that it was both innocent and spontaneous. This is one instance where the original is worth savoring, not copying.

There was another game upcoming, with archrivals Sweden and Finland colliding and a medal hanging in the balance, but it seemed more inconsequential than usual to the fans spilling out of the Olympic Arena after the Russian game. My first mission was, as usual, to meet Brooks in the arena manager's office. Brooks had not done any inquiring for potential coaching jobs after the Olympics and fully intended to return to the University of Minnesota, where Athletic Director Paul Giel, a former Minnesota football and baseball star, had adopted Brooks as his coach—forever. My favorite scene in *Miracle* is the one where the Brooks character slumps to the floor in the darkened arena corridor, overcome by emotion. Great scene. Didn't happen. Brooks was waiting for me in that arena office, and when I walked in, he was sitting behind the desk, grinning like a Cheshire cat. As I sat down in a chair facing him, the first words Brooks said were "This is going to cost Giel a ton!"

Hardly the words of a man overcome with emotion.

Outside in the gathering darkness, other journalists had finally figured out that they could catch the US players as they left the arena after having showered and changed. Only two problems: By then, they had to fight a throng of fans trying to do the same thing, and the media couldn't readily identify the players in civilian clothes. I interviewed John Harrington, and as I squeezed through the throng to find other players, I heard someone yell: "Mark . . . Hey, Mark." It was a *New York Times* reporter, thinking Harrington was Mark Johnson.

I found David Christian and asked if the cool demeanor meant the US was confident of hanging on. He replied, "In the last 10 minutes, they didn't even get a real good chance. Confident? I was confident when there were four seconds to go, and we had the puck."

Eruzione, who couldn't stop smiling, said, "If anyone had said we'd be going into the last period down one to the Russians, nobody would have believed it. . . . Everything we had to do to win, we did it. We just beat the best team in the world . . . No, wait, they're not. Maybe we are."

McClanahan picked up on that. "We beat the best team in the world, so maybe we're the best team in the world. We weren't as awed as we were in New York."

That made it flash through my mind that once again, something that looked like a mistake turned out to be an asset for the US, which had been able to ratchet up their performance to follow

Brooks's lead because of the memory of that humiliating 10–3 game, and maybe ratchet down their admiration for the Russians because of Brooks and his Stan Laurel routine.

Mark Johnson, with two of the four goals including the amazing buzzer beater, said: "What a great feeling. I can't tell you what it's like right now. Maybe in a few years, I'll sit back and be excited."

In later years, Johnson said if the teams played 100 times, the Russians would probably win 99 of them, "but we just happened to catch them in the 100th game."

Defenseman Billy Baker added, "It's just crazy. I still can't believe it. They weren't as physical this time, and Jimmy proved to be a big-time goalie. We all sang 'God Bless America' in the dressing room after the game, although we had to teach a few of the guys the words."

I barely had time to hammer out a lengthy but restrained game story, and a feature about the postgame scene outside the arena, suggesting that the nightly fireworks being shot off over nearby Mirror Lake on that particular night were really "bombs bursting in air," like the song says. And then I had that date to walk to the "Hostage House" to meet and talk to the US parents.

There was a priceless footnote to Al Michaels's game-closing statement. I read in later years various interviews with Michaels, including one in *Playboy* magazine's monthly interview, in which he told in great detail about how as he realized the chance grew for the US to spring the upset, he had to come up with a unique and impactful closing line, and so he formulated that one. Years later, I spotted two old friends sitting together after a big St. Paul hockey function, and they called me over. It was Keith "Huffer" Christiansen, former All-American at Minnesota-Duluth, and Mike "Lefty" Curran, former goaltender at the University of North Dakota, both of whom played at International Falls High School, and later with the Minnesota Fighting Saints in the World Hockey Association and on the 1972 Olympic team that won the silver medal in Sapporo, Japan.

They said that each player had been given videotapes of the broadcast from when they clinched the silver medal, behind the USSR's gold. As the final game ended, play-by-play announcer Curt Gowdy said, "Do you believe in miracles?"

The nugget Christiansen and Curran found interesting was when they learned that Gowdy's color man in 1972 at Sapporo was a young broadcaster named . . . Al Michaels.

Maybe, under the self-imposed pressure to find a great line, the powers of recall came through.

14

Mr. O Holds Court

NOTHING WAS CERTAIN EXCEPT 48 hours of euphoria for Team USA after defeating the Soviet Union, 4–3, in the next-to-last game of the 1980 Olympic hockey tournament. Engulfed in proper celebration by all the hard-core fans who made it to Lake Placid and filled the 8,100-seat Olympic Arena, it seemed difficult to realize Team USA would have to return in less than 48 hours to take on Finland, with the gold medal hanging in the balance.

While the crazed "U-S-A!, U-S-A!" chanters chanted outside, the action hadn't ended inside the arena. It took a while before word seeped out that Sweden had overturned a 2–0 deficit and vaulted ahead of Finland, 3–2, in the third period, but Finland's Mikko

Leinonen scored his second goal of the game, and the game ended 3–3.

It was still Friday night, and with a day off Saturday and only Sunday's final games to go, the US stood 1–0–1 against fellow medal-rounders, the USSR 1–1, Sweden 0–0–2, and Finland 0–1–1. The US could clinch the gold by beating Finland, but if Finland beat the US and the USSR beat Sweden, the USSR would end up 2–1 and take their umpteenth gold medal, while the US and Finland would both end 1–1–1, but Finland would get the silver by having beaten the US head-to-head.

Of less consequence except to the participants, Czechoslovakia— the favorite beaten 7–3 by the underdog US in Game 2—shocked Canada, 6–1, in the fifth-place game as Marian Stastny scored three goals and his brother Anton added two.

What all the partying fans didn't know was that when the US players disappeared, it was because they had a rare chance to celebrate with their parents. "There was a Holiday Inn a couple of blocks away, and they set up a place for us and our parents to get together and watch the replay of our game against the Russians," said Jack O'Callahan.

The players may have thought it was a special replay on their behalf, but it was actually another one of those details that broke for Team USA. The argument and mutual stubbornness that caused ABC to not switch programming and carry the US-Soviet game live, after being told the Olympic Committee would not switch the game to the night spot, caused ABC to videotape the game in the afternoon and broadcast it at 8:30 p.m. in the allotted time for Olympic coverage. Essentially, ABC put the game on nationwide for hockey fans everywhere, including the US players and their parents at the Holiday Inn in Lake Placid.

The timing was perfect for my writing duties, too. I had time to finish a major game story and a scene feature about standing outside in the snow and get everything sent to the *Minneapolis Tribune* with time to spare before walking a few blocks up the hill from the arena to the "Hostage House," a large and stately home that had been converted into about 10 rooms for rent during the Olympics.

O'Callahan had a hand in the colorful story of that large house, because he had presented his parents with a credit card and a reservation to spend two weeks at Lake Placid for the Olympics as a Christmas gift. When he got hurt in the exhibition game against the Russians, coach Herb Brooks said they would find him a place to stay if he couldn't play, and a room in that big house was what they found. His parents, who lived in Boston, said they might not go if Jack couldn't play. "I told them they were going anyway, because even if I couldn't play, this was my team, and these were the Olympics," Jack recalled. "It turned out they had the greatest time of their lives."

The house had been converted to about 10 rental rooms, and some other US players' family members were also there. "But after we tied Sweden and beat the Czechs, more and more parents showed up in Lake Placid to see us play, and they didn't have any place to stay," said O'Callahan. "In every case, one or more of the parents would invite them to come over to the house and said they could find a spare bed or a couch they could sleep on."

It wasn't long until there was an estimated 40 people living there, and that was the scene they had agreed to allow me to join for a large-scale group interview. I knew all the parents of the Gophers players, and several from the other Western college teams, but there were a half-dozen sets of parents I didn't know. They all welcomed me; with the US victory over the Russians fresh on everybody's mind, there were a lot of pleasantries to discuss. The parents, of course, saw it twice, once live and the second time on the ABC telecast with their sons.

At a huge dining room table, I took a seat near one end, and the parents filled the rest of the seats. There were the Verchotas from Duluth; the Silks from Boston; the Harringtons, Paveliches, Schneiders, and Bakers from the Iron Range; and others from the Minneapolis-St. Paul area. And then a little guy came in and sat to my left. He had a navy-blue knit cap, pulled down low to his eyeglasses, and he wore a coat, with the US team's insignia on the chest, and it was several sizes too big for him because it belonged to his son.

The other parents all got a kick out of "Mr. O"—John O'Callahan. Around Boston University's hockey team, he was also called Jack O'Callahan, which is the same name as his son, US defenseman Jack O'Callahan. Mr. O had a raspy voice, and that wonderful Boston accent, where he softened "Harvard" to "Hahvad," and you could tell from his first declaration that he loved to tell captivating stories.

But amid the afterglow of Team USA's huge victory, everybody went silent and focused their attention, when Mr. O looked around the table, then spoke.

"You know what the most important thing that happened tonight was?" he asked, with no intention of giving anyone the chance to answer. "Tonight, Billy Christian became David Christian's fah-thah! In the eyes of the world, no longer is David the son of Billy Christian. As of now, Billy Christian is David Christian's fah-thah!"

We all nodded, even though Billy Christian, from the Warroad Christians, never displayed any conceit for his accomplishments. It was true, however, that Billy Christian scored two goals against the Russians in the 1960 Olympics at Squaw Valley for the first and only US gold medal, then along with brother and 1960 teammate Roger Christian parlayed that fame into the long-standing Christian Brothers hockey stick company. So David Christian was raised being known as Billy Christian's son.

And Mr. O was right on in his assessment, that this victory over this Russian team would elevate David Christian to the status of the family's new celebrity.

In fact, every player on the US roster rose similarly to higher stature because of this triumph.

I knew of the Charlestown area in Boston, where the O'Callahans lived. It is a tough, uncompromising Irish community, and Mr. O put it in perspective for this group of mostly Minnesotans. "Charlestown is great," he said. "It's all Irish, and you know nobody hates the Irish like the Irish. You treat people right, they leave you alone; if you don't, they take care of you. Might blow you away. That's life in the big city."

Mr. O knew Mike Eruzione well, of course, because he lived nearby. "He lives in the Winthrop area, out in the water," he said. "They have a correctional institution there."

I told Mr. O that Eruzione told me, "I'm not from O'Callahan's hometown, but most of the kids from his hometown are in jail in my hometown."

Mr. O, still under that knitted cap and oversize jacket, laughed and said, "It's true. Half of Jackie's Pee Wee team is in jail. Jackie's a tough kid, but I raised him right."

With that, Mr. O launched into a colorful story about how he raised his kids, including Jackie, who grew to 6-foot-2, compared to his dad, who was 5-foot-6. He said he always told his kids if they ever thought they could take him, to say so, and they'd go downstairs and put the boxing gloves on. One day, Mr. O said, when

Jackie was 18, he said he thought he could take his dad, so they went downstairs. First, he said, he kicked Jackie in the groin, then "hit him with a good left—I'm left-handed." All of a sudden, Jackie was flat on his back, and Mr. O had his foot on Jackie's chest.

I looked around the table, and at least a dozen parents of other US players were wide-eyed and shocked. I asked Mr. O if he wouldn't fight clean against his own son.

"Fight clean?" he said. "You kidding? He's 6-1 and I'm 5-6. You think I survived growing up in Charlestown by fighting clean? No way. I fight dirty, man. That's how I made it. That's the way it is."

Dads named Strobel, Suter, Pavelich, and others laughed, but more out of disbelief. There are a lot of ways to raise your son, and everybody on this team seemed to have been raised right, so I didn't question Mr. O. I never forgot that story, either, and 40 years later I had the chance to ask Jack O'Callahan about the details.

"It never happened," Jack the younger said. "I want you to know, it never happened. My dad would never lay a hand on me, just like I would never lay a hand on my kids. But I'll tell you two things my dad loved to do—he loved to tell stories, and he loved to hold court. And he reeled you in, big-time."

While Jack went on to play for seven years in the NHL, mostly for the Chicago Blackhawks, he also started in the world of finance while playing, and when he retired from hockey, he was a founder and president of Beanpot Financial Services until he moved to a position of senior manager at Ziegler Capital Management (ZCM). He said he majored in American history at Boston U. but was always interested in financial management.

His parents remained for the rest of their lives in the Charlestown home where he grew up. A couple years after his mom died of a stroke, his dad complained about having a cold in January 2014, but it turned into pneumonia before he went in for treatment, and it claimed his life at age 82.

"They never moved from that house," Jack said. "They had a great life and my dad loved Charlestown. Both of them were healthy. My mom was healthy right up until she had a stroke, and my dad was healthy until his cold turned into pneumonia. But they had the greatest time of their lives at that house in Lake Placid. All those parents came together the way a good team might come together. They made friends for life.

"In fact, Herbie held a reunion for the parents at his home in Shoreview, and none of the players were invited. We were a close team, but it took us six months to come together. Our parents did it in five days."

CHAPTER 15

Finnish Finish

HAVING WATCHED FINLAND NEARLY BEAT the Russians during pool play and in a couple of other games, there was no doubt they represented a serious threat to Team USA in the final Olympic medal-round game. When I talked to a couple of US players on the day before they faced Finland, I told them they had an exceptional forward named Reijo Leppanen, the best of a skilled group, and some very good defensemen.

When I mentioned Leppanen, who had five goals and four assists in six games, pro scouts would always add the Finns also had Tepio Levo, who might be the best defenseman in the whole tournament. Nobody mentioned a couple 19-year-olds on the Finnish team, Jari Kurri and Reijo Ruotsalainen, who went on to have sensational

NHL careers, Kurri on right wing with Wayne Gretzky on Stanley Cup-winning Edmonton Oilers teams and Ruotsalainen on defense with the New York Rangers.

Flashing-forward to Sunday and the early medal-round game between Team USA and Finland—which was broadcast live by ABC television, by the way—the teams lined up for pregame introductions. The public address announcer at the Olympic Arena started out by saying that two players should be scratched from Finland's lineup, forward Reijo Leppanen and defenseman Tepio Levo.

Was that the final part to the magic? Leppanen suffered a pulled groin against Sweden in their first medal-round game, and Levo, Finland's best defenseman, suffered torn knee ligaments and was sent home to Finland to undergo surgery. Finland's best two players were not in their lineup. The Americans were still so pumped from beating the Russians that they didn't even know what Leppanen and Levo meant to the Finns.

The opening puck was dropped, and the Americans started rolling, with Mike Eruzione getting a good early shot, the Mark Johnson line following up during an early power play, and the Mark Pavelich Conehead Line creating a threatening shift. But the one disturbing trend the US had during the Olympics was that goaltender Jim Craig always played well, although often not until he had given up a peculiarly easy goal. And that happened again.

At 9:20 of the first period, Mikko Leinonen rushed up the left side and passed to his right to Jukka Porvari, a left-handed shooter playing right wing, as the Finns liked to do. Porvari wound up and, with no screen, fired a 50-foot blast that went in, about two feet in from the right post, and Finland led, 1–0. It was the sixth time in their seven games that the Americans gave up the first goal.

Before the period ended, Neal Broten sent the puck on net and Steve Christoff tipped it, and it hit fallen goaltender Jorma Valtonen and popped up and over him. Valtonen rolled over onto his back and got his glove on the puck, preventing the tying goal by about an inch. The US had a 14–7 edge in shots through the first period but trailed, 1–0. Maybe that was a good omen, because only in the romp against Romania had the US scored the first goal.

Early in the second period, Broten and Christoff were killing the end of a penalty to Mike Ramsey. Broten pestered a Finnish skater to free the puck, and Christoff raced in, cutting to the slot and scoring with a backhand at 4:39, two seconds after the penalty expired. But Buzzy Schneider drew another penalty at 6:00, and Mikko Leinonen broke in on the left side, dropping the puck back and then circling behind the net and out the other side just in time to bank in the return feed, and Finland was back in front, 2–1.

The US had several more good chances but misfired badly on a power play, and the second period ended with Finland still clinging to a 2–1 lead. After six months of preparation, a long and exhausting exhibition tour, and final bonding in time to knock off the powerful Soviet Union, here was Team USA looking at the last 20 minutes and at risk of forfeiting the gold medal for bronze if they couldn't overturn the 2–1 deficit against Finland.

To its credit, Team USA had shown no lack of poise while intensifying its attack late in the second period, and that momentum may have paid off in the third period. At 2:25, defenseman David Christian made an explosive rush up the middle into the Finland zone and passed to his left, where Phil Verchota, pretty much the forgotten force on the fourth line, collected the pass and drilled it into the net from the left circle, tying the game, 2–2.

At 6:05, Mark Johnson came over the boards on a line change and got the puck in behind the Finland net, while Rob McClanahan, his left wing, came on later and was possibly unnoticed by the Finnish defenders. McClanahan skated right to the net, wide open, took

Johnson's pass, and slid the puck under Valtonen. The US had taken its first lead in the game at 3–2 and celebrated as much with relief as excitement.

The game wasn't in hand just yet, though. Broten was called for hooking at 6:48, and Christian went off for tripping at 8:54, just after Broten got out. The penalty killers were put under a microscope, and Herb Brooks used a variety of combinations. Pavelich and Schneider went out first, then Johnson and McClanahan, while Jim Craig came up with some big saves in his typically solid third period. When they had to go right back to work, it was Christoff and Broten first out, then Pavelich and Schneider, concluding the two minutes with Johnson and McClanahan.

Verchota got whistled for roughing at 15:45, making it three straight penalties and five of the last six in the last two periods. Johnson and Christoff were up on the kill, with the US needing only to endure four more minutes to win the gold, and they did better than endure it. Christoff was forceful in taking over the puck and ramming it out of the US zone, where Johnson grabbed it at the blue line and raced all the way in for a shot. Valtonen blocked it, but Johnson got his own rebound and scored a short-handed goal with only 3:35 to go to make it 4–2, USA.

When the clock got into the last two minutes, somebody in the crowd bellowed, "We're number one!" igniting an immediate chant. Another guy pulled out a bugle and played "Charge." In the final minute, with no thought of backing off, Pavelich made two slick set-ups that weren't converted, but the puck was as far away from Craig and the US goal as it could be. The two-goal margin meant the totally drained crowd could finally relax, and the final seconds ticked away almost peacefully.

When it ended, Herb Brooks went to the auditorium/press center and brought the entire team for a mass interview session to celebrate the biggest surprise gold medal-winning performance in Winter Olympics history, finishing with a 6–0–1 record.

Brooks spoke first: "Much has been said about the players and press conferences, but you people have been watching a group of people who startled the athletic world—not just the hockey world. You people who are fathers might kick your sons in the ass a few times, and as coach, I did, too. You love your sons . . . as I love this hockey club."

Mark Johnson, who scored five goals—three in the medal round's two victories—to tie for the team lead with McClanahan and Schneider, said, "I'll probably wake up tomorrow morning and still not believe it. When we beat the Russians, we knew this sixty minutes would be the end of our season, the end of our hockey team. I just sit here in awe."

Craig said, "If anyone in here isn't surprised we won the gold medal, let me know. Every time we needed a big play, to block shots or win face-offs, these guys did it. If I told you guys not to block a shot, D [defensemen], thanks a lot. We had seven games in thirteen days, and six days of practice. The practices bothered me; the seven games were fun."

Craig added, "If any kid deserves a gold medal and got no playing time, but never did anything bad, pushed me all year, and is somebody I love, it's Steve Janaszak."

With that, the entire team rose in a standing ovation for the backup goaltender, who stayed ready and stayed positive but never got a minute of action.

A media person asked Eruzione, "Would you like to see this team stay together?" And Eruzione, the captain, replied, "I would like to take two weeks off, first. We jelled into a team in six months, and no coach or anyone else could have experienced the kind of season we've had. When we leave here, who knows if I'll ever see John

Harrington, or David Christian, again. That's a shame, and maybe a relief, too."

Jack O'Callahan came in late, with a beer in his hand, and jumped up on the table set up on the stage. "My question is to coach Brooks . . . " he began, triggering an immediate and jovial chorus of boos from the players. A media person asked Brooks, "Do you expect to be the coach again?" O'Callahan interrupted: "Gong that question!"

It was a lighthearted release of all the remaining energy the US players had.

O'Callahan, who hadn't gotten as much ice time as his mind wanted because his body couldn't take it, had the most energy and spent it as the closing headliner.

"I'm from Charlestown," O'Callahan said. "Charlestown is in the shadow of Bunker Hill. The Americans won at Bunker Hill, and the Americans won at Lake Placid . . . "

Somebody said, "The Americans didn't win at Bunker Hill."

"I don't want to hear that," O'Callahan shot back.

16

Reflections of a Miracle

THE POSTGAME CELEBRATION AFTER THE 4–2 victory over Finland took over the high school auditorium that had become the press center for all hockey interviews, and everybody had their chance to take part.

President Jimmy Carter had called after the Russia game to invite the team to the White House when the Olympics ended, and Vice President Walter Mondale attended in person when the US won the gold against Finland two days later. He came into the US dressing room afterward and, being from Minnesota, congratulated the players and asked, "How many of you are from Minnesota?"

Brooks intervened. "Nobody is from Minnesota, Mr. Vice President, we're all from the USA."

When all the players were on the auditorium's stage, they joked about one of their internal buzzwords being a "big doolie." Mike Eruzione said, "We're all big doolies now." Phil Verchota, laughing, explained that a big doolie is "a big wheel, or a big gun."

Somebody asked if the players could recount some of the "Brooksisms" they had heard about, and John Harrington came forward, because he had kept a notebook of some of the catchphrases Brooks used, over and over.

"You looked like a monkey [screwing] a football out there," Harrington began, continuing in rapid-fire fashion. "We're damned if we did and damned if we didn't. . . . Fool me once, shame on you; fool me twice, shame on me. . . . For lack of a better phrase . . . That about wraps it up . . . We reloaded and went up to the tiger and spit in his eye, and then we shot him. . . . We went to the well again, the water was colder and the water was deeper."

Somebody else asked if Harrington thought Brooks was a big doolie, and he paused, then said: "Yeah, he's a big doolie. A real big doolie." Then Harrington looked at Brooks and applauded, as the rest of the team joined in.

Later, I was able to get one last exclusive talk with Brooks, and he let his emotions guide a scattershot conversation. "I got a call from the New York Rangers, and they said, 'Don't make a move without talking to us.' They made me an offer. I turned it down," Brooks said.

"We're tired physically and tired mentally. Seven games in thirteen days, and in six of the seven the other team got the first goal. We gave up nine goals in the first period, but we only had three goals against in the second period and three goals against in the third period through all seven games," said Brooks, taking obvious pride in his team's strength and conditioning advantage he had been striving for all year, concluding with blanking both Finland and the USSR in the third periods of the two medal-round conquests. According to Brooks, Harrington said, "There's a method to your madness."

"I felt we'd have to grind this one out against Finland, and suck it up," Brooks said. We got a pretty good game out of Christoff, his best of the tournament, by far. . . . I was going to get a haircut this morning, but I just didn't have time. . . . Screw New York! Maybe I'll be coaching Bantams in Mounds View next year. If I got a job coaching in the NHL, I would insist on playing a system like this. We played better as we gained experience playing this style, and I would do it in the NHL, even if it cost me. I'd do it and let them fire me."

Brooks said he didn't go onto the ice to join the celebration after the Finland game, because that was the players' time. "I went right to the dressing room," he said. "I bit 'em right up until the end, and I didn't want to intrude on their celebration."

We got the word that out on the Olympic Arena ice, in the game between the two No. 1 seeds that was anticipated to be for the gold medal, the Soviet Union defeated Sweden, 9–2. That nine-goal onslaught is what the US would have had to confront if Brooks had gotten his wish to face the Russians in the last game, rather than the next-to-last one. Just another part of the magical guidance that governed Team USA.

Years later, when Mark Johnson was becoming the most successful coach in women's hockey at The University of Wisconsin-Madison, his alma mater, we had occasion to talk often during the WCHA women's season. Mark looked back and said, "If we played the Russians 100 times, they probably would have won 99 of the games. We just happened to catch them in the other one."

Johnson was right, that it would take a few years to see the gold medal in proper perspective. But that night, after beating Finland

and joining the whole team when captain Mike Eruzione motioned them all to join him on the top pedestal at the medal ceremony in the arena, the emotion of it all was never-ending.

Afterward, Brooks turned introspective. Bob Fleming, from AHAUS, the Amateur Hockey Association of the US—later shortened to USA Hockey—and always a supporter of Brooks in the ongoing ideological disagreements he had with the organizing body, joined us briefly.

"Unbelievable that a college team wins the Olympic gold," said Brooks. "Unbelievable, unbelievable . . . I was good after the game until my wife started crying, then I started crying," Brooks added.

Bob Fleming said: "You might be human, after all."

I asked Brooks if the players saw him crying, and he said, "No, I cried the other way."

Each team gets 20 medals, and there are 20 players on the active roster, a point that Brooks noted.

"Helluva deal," he said. "I missed one in 1960, and now I missed another one in 1980. It's ironic that 20 years later I'm here, in a different role. I talked to Jack McCartan here, and he said, 'Herb, it's meant to be. It'll happen.' He was the last guy I talked to in 1960, in the Denver arena after I was the last guy cut. The team went one way, to Squaw Valley, and I went the other—home."

Brooks was set to be on the 1960 team, amid John Mayasich, Tommy Williams, Billy and Roger Christian, and Bill Cleary, who remained a close friend of Brooks during his long coaching career at Harvard. It was Cleary who pulled the power play that proved pivotal. One of the best players on the team, Cleary said his brother, Bob Cleary, should be on the team, and if coach Jack Riley didn't take him, then he would quit the team. Maybe it was just a high-pressure gambit, but Riley gave in, giving the team the Christian brothers and the Cleary brothers. But in the process, one player had to be cut, and that was Brooks.

"I called my dad when I got the news," Brooks recalled, in that Lake Placid setting. "My dad said, 'Keep your mouth shut, thank the coach, wish the players luck, and come home.' I remember sitting with my dad, watching on TV as the US won the gold medal at Squaw Valley, and my dad said, 'Well, it looks like they cut the right guy.'"

Billy Cleary was the first coach asked to coach the 1980 US team, but he turned it down—a forgotten irony to be added to the total picture.

"It's funny, but I feel a little let down," Brooks confided. "I went through nine or ten months preparation before the Sports Festival, then we had six more months to get to Lake Placid. Now everybody will be gone. Everybody splits. But as years go by, this will mean more to them.

"The players were singing 'God Bless America' over and over in the dressing room. They were all laughing and crying. I don't think I'll ever witness anything like it."

In the auditorium, after the mass press conference with all the US players, they all trooped out of the building to the waiting crowd of fans. The entire body of reporters all shamelessly trooped out after them, trying to get one last priceless comment. Too bad, because they were practically rude about completely ignoring the contingent from Finland, which had been patiently waiting to take their turn onstage.

There was one television crew from Finland, with an announcer and cameraman, and me attending the final talk with Frank Moberg, one of the Finnish coaches and the spokesman for the program.

"Getting to the medal round was something new for Finland,"

he said. "We expected a lot of noise for the home team, but I admire the way they support their team. The USA has the gold medal, and the Soviet team has something else, so the US team is better. We knew before the tournament that the US had a good team, and as the tournament progressed, it became evident it was a really good team. And now, obviously, they are the best.

"They work hard, skate hard, and have some European elements to their game. They have more diverse style than the NHL teams show. We hope to keep our team together for the World Championships next year, but there are guys with a lot of money watching our team for two weeks here. We think we have by far a better conditioned team than most North American teams, and our average age is just under twenty-three."

True enough, players like Jari Kurri and Reijo Ruotsalainen led a movement of top Finnish players to lucrative NHL careers, so Moberg was prophetic. In evaluating the whole Winter Olympic tournament, he again returned to what he had observed. But it wasn't until the 2019 World Championships, in Moscow, that Finland rose to the highest echelon of international hockey. With NHL professionals dominating the US, as well as Sweden, Russia, and Canada—the three favorites—Finland, with no NHL players, defeated Sweden, Russia, and Canada in the quarterfinals, semifinals, and final to win its first world championship. The Finnish program, which only 40 years earlier had declared that it had no chance to beat the Russians, picked up an entirely new and different attitude, and confidence. And it's possible that the inspiration might have come in some small way from Team USA in 1980.

"It is a small surprise that the US won the gold medal," Moberg said, back at Lake Placid. "I say small, because we had the Russians wondering for a while, and Canada had the Russians in trouble.

"But the US works real hard, and they hustle, and they have this
. . . this *spirit*," Moberg said, reaching out with his hand to gesture.
"You can almost touch it."

17

The Real World

TIME STOOD STILL FOR EVERYBODY connected with Team USA in 1980 at Lake Placid, leaving indelible memories and lasting fame. Some players moved right into professional hockey and went onward and upward, others stayed involved in the game in some manner, and still others went off into private business with varying degrees of success. Some, as of 2020, will have already retired after productive careers.

Whenever any of them get together or just run into one another, none of that matters. All that matters is the special bond from sharing seven months together in close proximity, learning one another's personalities and habits, and becoming, genuinely, a family.

Herb Brooks, the organizer, selector, choreographer, strategist, motivator, manipulator and hard-driving coach who extracted the best out of all 20 of his players, had a brilliant seven-year coaching career at the University of Minnesota, winning NCAA championships in 1974, 1976, and 1979 before taking on the project of Team USA for the 1980 Winter Games. Brooks went on to coach a team in Davos, Switzerland, the year after Lake Placid, which may have been part of fulfilling a lifelong fantasy about living and working in the Swiss Alps, where one of his all-time favorite movies, *The Sound of Music*, was based.

Brooks returned to North America for a chance to coach the New York Rangers in the National Hockey League. He coached there four years, and by establishing records of 39–27–14, 35–35–10, and 42–29–9 in his first three years he earned the honor of winning 100 games sooner than any other Rangers coach. He went from Manhattan back to Minnesota to coach one injury-filled season with the North Stars in 1987–88 and later coached the New Jersey Devils for the 1992–93 season. He took over the Pittsburgh Penguins for part of the 1999–2000 season for his former protégé and assistant, Craig Patrick, who was general manager. His seven seasons of NHL coaching produced a 219–219–66 record.

Brooks also set out to fulfill the objective of his coach and mentor at the University of Minnesota, John Mariucci, to help expand Division I hockey to other hockey-playing state colleges beyond Minnesota and Minnesota-Duluth. Mariucci always thought that Minnesota, with the wellspring of youth hockey prospects through its high school program, should expand to St. Cloud State, Minnesota State-Mankato, and Bemidji State. Brooks took on St. Cloud State as a personal project, speaking at state legislature functions to get financial backing for an arena complex on the St. Cloud campus, where he would take over as coach to guide the transition from Division II up to Division I.

His legacy has been maintained despite the breakup of the old Western Collegiate Hockey Association. Minnesota went off to play in the newly formed Big Ten Conference, UMD and St. Cloud joined the newly formed National Collegiate Hockey Conference, and MSU-Mankato and Bemidji State remained in the shattered WCHA. And yet all were thriving, as the 2019–20 season began, with UMD seeking its third straight NCAA championship, while St. Cloud State was out to defend its regular-season NCHC championship and MSU-Mankato was defending champion of the WCHA.

Brooks also agreed to an arrangement to coach in France, where he was hired to try to make the French Olympic team into a valid competitor. Without speaking any French, he assembled and trained a team in a short period of time, and they entered the World Championships, where they won an astonishing 1998 upset over the US, which relegated the Americans to have to play its way back up to Olympic stature. Brooks noted that the players in France enjoyed playing games but never had structured coaching or practices. France finished 11th in the 1998 Winter Olympics but made almost every game competitively closer than at any time before or since.

By that time, old rivalries and disagreements between Brooks and USA Hockey (formerly AHAUS) had subsided, and Brooks was hired to coach Team USA's new crop of NHL pro stars in the 2002 Winter Olympics at Salt Lake City. The players had precious little time away from NHL games to be organized or practice, but Brooks coordinated them impressively. The team went undefeated through the preliminary round and into the medal round, which was by then rearranged into an eight-team bracket instead of round robin. The US defeated a very strong Russian team in the semifinals.

Star players included forwards Brett Hull, Mike Modano, Jeremy Roenick, Chris Drury, Bill Guerin, Keith Tkachuk, John LeClair, Brian Rolston, Tony Amonte, Mike York, and Adam Deadmarsh; defensemen Brian Leetch, Phil Housley, Chris Chelios, Brian Rafalski, Aaron Miller, Tom Poti, and Gary Suter; and goaltenders Mike Richter, Tom Barrasso, and Mike Dunham. The US had to settle for the silver medal when they lost the gold to Canada, managed by Wayne Gretzky and coached by Pat Quinn, with a star-studded lineup that included forwards Mario Lemieux, Jarome Iginla, Eric Lindros, Joe Sakic, Brendan Shanahan, Paul Kariya, Theo Fleury, and Steve Yzerman; defensemen Al MacInnis, Chris Pronger, Scott Niedermayer, Rob Blake, Eric Brewer, and Ed Jovanovski; and goalies Martin Brodeur, Curtis Joseph, and Ed Belfour. The loss to Canada was the only loss in two Olympic tournaments for Brooks. The NHL stars on Team USA, such as Hull and Modano, expressed great appreciation for the unique—but comparatively laid-back—coaching brilliance of Brooks in their brief relationship. Hull said if he were to sign another NHL contract, he would want a stipulation that insisted Brooks be hired as coach.

Brooks had plans to continue his remarkable career, dedicating his boundless energy to being director of scouting for the Penguins and expanding his unique coaching concepts into a youth coaching plan that he devised with Jack Blatherwick, which would aid in developing young players to play what he foresaw as a unique "American style." But Brooks's life was tragically cut short by a highway crash in 2003. He was driving his minivan home from a hockey-golf fundraiser on the Iron Range because he had an out-of-town speaking engagement. He apparently lost control and over-corrected his minivan, which rolled over several times. Brooks was killed instantly, at 66, on August 11, 2003. The hockey arena at St. Cloud State that he had arranged, along with an adjacent practice rink—both of Olympic 200x100 proportions—were renamed in his honor.

Having played at the University of Minnesota, Brooks played on US Olympic teams in 1964, at Innsbruck, Austria, and 1968, when he was captain of the team at Grenoble, France. He also played on five US National teams, in 1961, 1962, 1965, 1967, and 1970. That gave him more than the basic appreciation for the European approach to hockey, and to his later coaching career, where first his iconic college tenure from 1972 to 1979 led to Team USA's perfect experiment, and later forays into the NHL.

When he was coaching the New Jersey Devils under general manager Lou Lamoriello in 1992–93, a decade after his time with the New York Rangers, I had the chance to sit down with Brooks for an interview at Brendan Byrne Arena, where he reflected back on 1980 and touched on the current status of the NHL and its prospective future.

"When I started with the Rangers, Edmonton [with Wayne Gretzky] and ourselves were the only teams that believed in a hybrid system, and a lot of hockey people second-guessed us," Brooks recalled. "I don't begrudge any other person's philosophy, but I took offense at being criticized for deviating at all from the mainstream. It's a better game for the players, and I believe in the ability of NHL players—on the ice, not the blackboard. No amount of upper-body strength can replace skating ability.

"The NHL is using the Olympic games to market their athletes, so I'd like to see the NHL eliminate the red line except for icing, and move the end lines out to 15 feet to open up the corners and take care of the congestion in the corners. The better players deserve an environment where they have room to come out and make plays.

"We're doing something different, trying a few things to use the total ice sheet, and looking at it all from a completely different physiological way, all geared to up-tempo play. To do creative stuff, you've got to make quick reads and make good decisions. Once the players learn it, they'll have a better chance for success in April and May. The problem is getting to April and May. I'd have a whole different philosophy if the Stanley Cup was played in October."

Brooks had a variety of players from a variety of countries on that Devils team, and he was looking to the future. "Pro hockey should be the most entertaining sport," he said, "because it's the fastest game, with a physical twist. The 1980s were real different than the '70s, and the '90s will be real different again. Teams have got to find different ways to beat the norm.

"I'm a traditionalist in a lot of things, like intensity, and the ability to adhere to transitions to offense, but I've always thought that being able to make quick transitions to defense might be the most valuable. I used the word transition in New York and was subjected to some ridicule, but I believe that offense is more personality, while defense is more character.

"It's such an elusive thing, and I'm always looking for more ways to find it. There are certain ideals to develop, but the pragmatics are that you've got to stay alive. We've got some good players, like Peter Stastny and Bobby Holik, and defensemen both young, in Scott Niedermayer, and experienced, in Russian star Viacheslav Fetisov—I just don't know how far we can go. We've got to get our defensemen involved in the offense, not necessarily lead the rush but be in the rush. There's no sense giving the puck to three forwards and then have them turn it over to five defenders on the other team. They always ran into a red light before. I've sort of gotten it to yellow, but we're not to green yet."

Getting the light to green was what Brooks accomplished with Team USA for 1980, but with the pros, putting such a concept together required unlearning a lot of previous rules. "We're consistently inconsistent," Brooks said. "I've been challenging them. They've got to be put on a cliff to have their comfort zone driven up. We could shut this thing down and go to north-south stuff, but we're not going to grow that way. I'd like to get them to play all styles—bump and grind, up-tempo, and dump and chase."

Brooks brought in Jack Blatherwick to institute training techniques, and Lamoriello, who had been an outstanding coach at Providence in college hockey, gave the new project full backing as general manager. "Every team wants to have a system where everybody works together," said Lamoriello. "Some teams try to force it, and it won't work for them. No question, that was part of my interest in going after Herb, because of his love for teaching the progressive style of hockey. Herb attacks the neutral zone and works from there to the offensive and defensive zones.

"I never saw a guy enjoy coaching as much as Herb. Perfection is part of his vocabulary, and he has his thoughts on how the game should be played. The biggest adjustment I've seen in Herb in one season is that he has a little more patience."

Brooks then, in 1993, recalled starting as a player in college.

"I was pretty much a traditionalist," he said. "Then I became enamored with the Russian and European influence. I'd watch a game and say, 'Wow,' or 'Geez,' but I was still a traditionalist. Then I watched in 1972 when the Russians played the series with the NHL All-Stars. All of a sudden, I realized there was another way to do it. It gave me a better perspective, but if you deviated from the North American style, they looked at you funny. In basketball and football, new ideas were fine, but not hockey.

"I was striving for the best parts of both Canadian and European hockey, trying for the best of both worlds. I started to do some of it with the Gophers, and then with the '80 Olympic team, I let it all hang out. I did some things with that team that I haven't done since."

But it was different with pros, even though Brooks's ideals were the same. "My philosophy has always been out of respect to the athletes' ability, and they're capable of a lot. With great athletes, you like to give the game to them, but they have to be responsible without the puck. Some who fit best are the Canadian pros, because they have such great instincts. Now we have Russians, Czechs, Finns, Swedes, Americans, and Canadians—it doesn't matter where you're from."

The biggest challenge coaches face, Brooks added, was that even if they have progressive ideas, they might have to back off in order to eke out enough wins to keep their jobs.

"You can't be liberal and aggressive as a coach when you're fighting for your life all the time," he said.

Brooks also missed his family, which mostly stayed back in Minnesota. And he could still fall back on some favorite lines. "If I could find Patti a penthouse on Fifth Avenue, everything would probably be better," he said.

"The last time she came out to visit, she had her credit cards stolen. I haven't reported it yet, though, because the thief is spending about $500 a month less than she was."

The influence Brooks had on NHL teams in New York, Minnesota, New Jersey, and Pittsburgh may have helped spur the game forward, as did the continuing influx of European players and arrival of more US players. He had gained great levels of sophistication—and patience—from the pros, particularly since his college coaching days, but listening to him talk about what happened more than a decade earlier was pretty convincing. Letting it all hang out with Team USA in 1980 at Lake Placid proved even to Brooks that there was another way to play the game.

18

Distant Perspective

OF ALL THE RECOLLECTIONS THE players on Team USA might have the most trouble with was the view from above, looking down on the ice surface from the press box at Lake Placid at the three teams assembled on the ice to receive their medals for the hockey tournament. The players couldn't see the overview, because they were down there, on the ice, in their stylish outfits.

One one side were the players from the Soviet Union, and on the other were the players from Sweden. In the middle were the players from the US, and they were much more in the mood to go celebrate their gold medal-winning performance in the 4–2 victory over Finland than to go through any more formalities. The Soviet players had crushed Sweden, 9–2, to win silver in the battle of the two top seeds, while the seventh-seeded Americans cruised in and swiped the gold.

In the jubilation of the moment, the US players shared the emotion with one another, one final time, as the officials of the Olympic Committee summoned each player from the bronze medal-winning Swedish team up to the pedestal to have the medals draped around their necks, then the Soviet Union team did the same to receive the silver medals.

When it came time for Team USA to get the gold medals, they hurried across the ice and climbed up onto the pedestal, one after the other, until they all had received their medals. Then captain Mike Eruzione climbed up for the team award, and when he was done, instead of climbing down, he waved to his teammates and gestured for them to come out and join him. In one of the memorable moments of the 1980 Winter Olympics, 20 hockey players all made it up onto the small pedestal designed for one.

It was a fitting finish for a team that came together as one, and the players were pretty much overwhelmed by the moment to appreciate what they had done. In Game 1, the Americans fell behind 1–0 and 2–1 before getting the pivotal 2–2 tie with 27 seconds to play. In Game 2, Czechoslovakia took an early 1–0 lead before Team USA gained a 2–2 tie and romped, 7–3. In Game 3, Norway struck first and held a 1–0 lead until the US scored three in the second and went on to win, 5–1. In Game 4, the US scored first, last, and in between to win, 7–2, in the only game where the Americans scored first. In Game 5, West Germany scored early and led, 2–0, into the second period before the US rallied to win, 4–2. On into the medal round, the Russians scored first and held leads of 1–0, 2–1, and 3–2, but the US came back for the Miracle 4–3 victory. In Game 7, Finland led, 1–0, after one period and 2–1 after two, before the rallying US gained the 4–2 victory to secure the gold medal.

Mike Ramsey, who was 19 when he starred on defense in 1980, had only finished his freshman year at the University of Minnesota, and he went directly into the Buffalo Sabres lineup, having signed with Scotty Bowman. After a long NHL career, he went into coaching, first at Buffalo, where he started with the Sabres, assisting his former teammate Lindy Ruff. He came home to Minnesota to join the Minnesota Wild expansion team staff and stayed there until retiring so he could watch his daughter and son grow up and play college hockey.

"I've gotten back to Lake Placid a few times," Ramsey said, in the summer of 2019. One of those times was in 2005, when they renamed the arena in honor of the late Herb Brooks.

"It hasn't changed much. You walk in, and you get that old feeling. The locker rooms are still the same. It's a long time to look back. I was 19, and I remember trying out and thinking I was too young to make it. Obviously, I was wrong."

The feeling persists that the NHL has resisted change and certainly didn't embrace going to the style of Team USA.

"But the game has changed a lot," Ramsey said. "Every team is so well coached now that it has become structured to the point where every mistake leads to a scoring chance. You drill and drill about how a player must be right here, in this situation, or right there, in that one.

"It is really hard to win, not only games, but championships, in the NHL. As a player and a coach, I was involved for 31 years, and I never won a Stanley Cup. And it's a fact that no matter how good you are through the long regular season, the only thing that matters to the players is who wins the Cup. Every team I was with worked and struggled to win it, but it's hard to win.

"A couple of years ago, Tampa upset a string of opponents and went all the way to win the Cup. All I could think of was, 'No!

You've got to struggle first!' It's not right to just put a new team together and win the Cup."

For others, the game was less accommodating. Billy Baker, who played defense as well, tried his hand at the NHL game, but it didn't fit, and he returned to go to dental school at the University of Minnesota and had an outstanding career as a dental surgeon in Brainerd, Minnesota.

Baker had the same feelings of uncertainty as all the US players from back at the National Sports Festival in 1979. The players recalled that Brooks was more than fair, the way he didn't take several marginal players, if they had promising work or pro offers. All the players were wondering if they would be cut. So Baker thought maybe he would show his hand in case he was in the "marginal" group.

"When Herb asked me about going to the sports festival, I said, 'You know, I've already been accepted into dental school,'" Baker said. "He didn't even look up."

That was part of the magic, that Baker and Ramsey, two ex-Gophers who still go hunting and fishing together regularly, represent the extremes of pro hockey careers, but they share the lifetime of camaraderie from Team USA. They joined all their teammates at Lake Placid in 2005 when they renamed the hockey arena in honor of Herb Brooks, who had died in 2003.

Here is a rundown of what has happened in the real world, as of late 2019, to the 1980 Team USA players, in numerical order of their jerseys:

1.   Steve Janaszak, White Bear Lake, Minnesota, goaltender. The only player on the roster to not play even a single minute, Janaszak had played starring roles at Hill-Murray High School on a state championship team and on the University of Minnesota's 1979 championship team. He joked that he got a gold medal for his backup role and

a silver lining because he met his wife at Lake Placid. Always quiet and consistent, he became a security blanket for Jim Craig and coach Herb Brooks. After the Olympics, he signed a pro contract with the Minnesota North Stars and later played briefly for the Colorado Rockies, but when an NHL opportunity wasn't forthcoming, he retired in 1982 to become an investment banker in New York.

3. Ken Morrow, Flint, Michigan, star defenseman at Bowling Green. At 6-foot-4, 205 pounds, Morrow was a force on the blueline, especially when injuries thinned the corps to basically four defensemen through the Olympic Games. He had been drafted in 1976 by the New York Islanders, and after the Olympics, he took his gold medal to New York, where he signed with the Islanders in time to help them win their first of four straight Stanley Cups. He became the first player to win the Olympic gold medal and the Stanley Cup in the same season. He also played for the US in the 1981 Canada Cup. He had knee problems that twice led to arthroscopic surgery and eventually shortened his career. After the season ended in 1989, he retired and became a scout and an assistant coach before being named director of pro scouting in 1993.

5. Mike Ramsey, Minneapolis, Minnesota, at 6-foot-3, became a standout right out of Roosevelt High School on the 1978–79 NCAA champion Gophers and was a forceful, smart defenseman who, while still a teenager at 19, paired with Morrow on the basic four-man rotation and was on the ice in the chilling last minute of the 4–3 victory over the Soviet Union. He immediately joined the Buffalo Sabres, where Scotty Bowman had drafted him 11th overall in 1979 and went on to play 1,070 NHL games for the Sabres, Pittsburgh Penguins, and Detroit Red Wings before ending an 18-year career to become assistant coach with the Sabres. He later was assistant to Jacques Lemaire with the Minnesota Wild before retiring to watch his daughter and son play hockey in high school and then at the University of Minnesota.

6. Bill Baker, Grand Rapids, Minnesota, stalwart 6-foot-1 defenseman who led the Gophers to the 1976 and 1979 NCAA titles, captain of the '79 team. Drafted by Montreal, he signed, and after a brief try at pro hockey with Montreal, the Colorado Rockies, St. Louis, and the New York Rangers, he retired and returned to the University of Minnesota and became an oral surgeon. He and his wife, Diane, moved to the Brainerd, Minnesota, area where he and some partners started an oral surgery business with multiple outlets, where he specialized in maxillofacial surgery. He sold his share of the business and retired. His No. 6 jersey is part of a permanent display at the Smithsonian Museum in Washington, DC.

7. Rob McClanahan, North Oaks, Minnesota, wing who was a junior speedster on the 1979 Minnesota NCAA championship team, followed Brooks onto the Olympic team, and played 224 NHL games with Buffalo, Hartford, and the New York Rangers before retiring and going into the investment banking business in the Minneapolis area. His daughter got a scholarship to play at the University of New Hampshire.

8. Dave Silk, Scituate, Massachusetts, star wing for Boston University and solid contributor in Brooks's "modular" forward style. Went on to play seven years of NHL hockey with the New York Rangers, Boston, Detroit, and Winnipeg and played in Europe until 1991, when he returned home and became an assistant coach at BU. He got out of hockey to go into investment banking in Boston.

9. Neal Broten, Roseau, Minnesota, a skilled, intuitive center whom Brooks recruited to Minnesota and immediately declared Broten was the most talented player he had ever coached. Broten concluded his freshman year by scoring a spectacular goal in the NCAA championship game that stood up as the game-winner against North Dakota for the 1979 title. After a strong Olympic showing, he returned to the University of Minnesota to play alongside his brother, Aaron Broten, and after the Gophers were upset by Wisconsin in the NCAA championship game, Broten was named winner of the first Hobey Baker Award, given to the nation's top player. He then signed with the Minnesota North Stars, who drafted him in the second round of the 1979 draft, and he played 13 years with them and parts of three seasons after the team moved to Dallas. He also played with the Los Angeles Kings and the New Jersey Devils, where he won a Stanley Cup in 1995. Played 1,099 games altogether in the NHL, scoring 289 goals and 634 assists for 923 points. Moved with his wife, Sally, to River Falls, Wisconsin, where they raise horses.

10. Mark Johnson, born in Minneapolis and raised in Madison, Wisconsin, the highly-skilled 5-foot-10 center scored at least one point in all seven Olympic games, including two goals against the Soviet Union in the 4–3 Miracle on Ice game, and a goal and an assist in the third-period rally to beat Finland, 4–2, in the gold medal finale. He led Team USA with 5–6–11 in the seven Olympic games and led the way all season with 38–54–92 in 60 games. He scored five goals as a teenager for the 1976 US Olympic team coached by his dad, Badger Bob Johnson, then starred for his dad for three seasons at the University of Wisconsin, where he tallied 36–44–80 as a freshman in 1976–77, when the Badgers won the NCAA title, and he was All-America with 48–38–86 in 1977–78, and again after scoring 41–49–90 in 1978–79, when he also was named college player of the year, before the Hobey Baker Award was awarded. After 1980, he played three seasons with Pittsburgh, and later with the North Stars, Hartford, St. Louis, and his final five seasons with New Jersey. After 669 games in the NHL, he played in both Milan, Italy, and in Austria before returning to Madison to go into coaching. He coached Madison Memorial High School for the 1993–94 season, then served as Jeff Sauer's assistant for six seasons with Wisconsin's men's team, before becoming head coach of the Badgers' women's program in 2003. He led the Badgers to back-to-back NCAA championships in 2006 and 2007 and had a total of five going into an attempt to defend its 2019 title, having already established himself as the winningest coach in women's hockey history.

11. Steve Christoff, right wing, Richfield, Minnesota, signed with the hometown North Stars after the Olympics and showed an explosive scoring touch by immediately setting a rookie record with eight goals in the playoffs. He suffered a broken collarbone in training camp before his second season, causing him to miss 24 games, and after his third season was traded to Calgary, then to the Los Angeles Kings before retiring in 1984 to pursue another of his passions—flying. He became an airline pilot, flying mostly for Endeavor Airlines, a regional subsidiary of Delta, in the Upper Midwest, and was still at it in 2019.

15. Mark Wells, center, St. Clair Shores, Michigan, star at Bowling Green from 1975 to 1979. At 5-foot-9, he had no scholarship offers, so he walked on at Bowling Green and used his quickness to become a prominent center, scoring 77 goals in his four years. He earned a scholarship after his freshman year, and after completing his eligibility, he joined teammate Ken Morrow on the 1980 US roster. A smart, two-way, right-handed center, he fit into the forward scheme, mainly centering the fourth line. After the gold medal, he signed with the Montreal Canadiens and played for two seasons at Nova Scotia and the New Haven Nighthawks of the AHL but retired without ever playing an NHL game. He worked as a restaurant manager in Rochester Hills, Michigan, but suffered a severe injury while unloading crates, fracturing a vertebra. After 11 hours of surgery, he was told he had a rare degenerative spinal ailment, which led to multiple surgeries and left him bedridden. In 2010, he sold his gold medal for $40,000 to a private collector to pay medical expenses, and the buyer reportedly sold it at auction for $310,700. He had recovered sufficiently by 2014 to make speaking engagements in St. Clair Shores.

16. Mark Pavelich, center, Eveleth, Minnesota, an All-American at Minnesota-Duluth, "Pav" centered the "Conehead Line" with UMD teammate John Harrington and Buzzy Schneider, remaining intact amid all the juggling on other lines. His passes always seemed to ignite rallies or win games, such as his feed to Billy Baker for the tying goal in the 2–2 opening game against favored Sweden; and, after setting up Schneider for the first goal against the Soviet Union, he passed the puck to the slot for Mike Eruzione's 4–3 game-winner against the USSR. Played briefly in Europe, then became an NHL star for the New York Rangers when Brooks coached there. He retired when Brooks was dismissed and returned to Minnesota's North Shore, where he worked in land development. He sent his gold medal to be auctioned off, and it sold for $202,900 in 2014, a move he said he made to secure his daughter's future.

17. Jack O'Callahan, defense, Charlestown, Massachusetts, made a remarkable comeback after tearing left knee ligaments in the 10–3 exhibition loss to the Soviet Union in Madison Square Garden. Doctors were divided on whether he could regain use of his leg in time, but Brooks made the 11th-hour decision to keep the former Boston University standout on the active roster. He missed the first two games, dressed but didn't play in the third game, then played in a part-time role on the third defense pairing against Romania, West Germany, briefly against the USSR, and in the gold medal-winning game against Finland. Afterward, he played NHL hockey with the Chicago Blackhawks for five years, and two more for New Jersey, and after 389 NHL games he began working in the financial business in Chicago in 1984 and became part-owner and president of Beanpot Financial, which he later sold, becoming senior manager of financial development for Ziegler Capital management.

19. Eric Strobel, right wing, Rochester, Minnesota, long-striding speedster who played on the 1979 Minnesota NCAA champs, scoring 30 goals on that prolific Gophers team, and he played a solid role on Team USA. He signed with the Buffalo Sabres after the Olympics, hoping to follow the footsteps of his father, who had played for the New York Rangers. The Sabres sent him to their Rochester Americans AHL affiliate, and after one month, he suffered a broken ankle. He came back the following season and played briefly in Baltimore before deciding to retire and return to college to get his degree. He went into business as a telephone sales executive and lives in Apple Valley, a Minneapolis suburb, where he has overcome the effects of a stroke and returned to business.

20. Bob Suter, Madison, Wisconsin, died of a heart attack in 2014 at age 57, while at Capital Arena in Madison. It was a shock to all, as he was serving as a scout for the Minnesota Wild, for whom his son,

Ryan Suter, played as one of the NHL's top defensemen. As a player, the 5-foot-9, 178-pound defenseman had an intense spirit that made a lasting impression on teammates, while opponents hated to play against him—characteristics not lost on Herb Brooks. His speed and dynamic impact were unfortunately limited after he suffered a broken ankle that caused him to miss much of the exhibition season, and he never got back to 100 percent in the Olympics. Though small, he was a tenacious competitor who helped Wisconsin win the 1977 NCAA championship. Suter signed a free-agent contract with the Minnesota North Stars after the Olympics but retired after one year in the minor leagues and returned to Madison, where he opened a sporting goods shop and worked with youth hockey development. His younger brother, Gary Suter, played 17 NHL seasons and on two Olympic teams, winning a silver medal on the 2002 Salt Lake City team coached by Herb Brooks.

21. Mike Eruzione, left wing, Winthrop, Massachusetts. The team captain came back from being on the bubble of being cut just before the Olympics started and wound up scoring the deciding goal in the 4–3 victory over the Soviet Union, for the "Miracle on Ice." A former Boston University standout, he played on the 1975 and 1976 US teams in the World Championships, where he famously dozed off as the hastily assembled 1976 team departed on a commercial flight for the Katowice, Poland, tournament and was asleep when coach John Mariucci sent a legal pad around for all the players to put down the position they wanted to play. He ended up as a bewildered spare as the US went 3–6–1 to place fourth, but teammates praised Eruzione's enthusiasm to Herb Brooks, which gained him an invitation to the 1980 tryouts, after playing for the Toledo Goaldiggers in the IHL. Teammates joke about Eruzione riding the fame of his huge goal to beat the USSR to never working in later years, when Eruzione has been a motivational speaker; has appeared on ABC, CBS, Fox, and USA networks; and became director of special outreach at BU.

23. David Christian, defenseman, Warroad, Minnesota, from a family with a lasting heritage from the tiny town on the Lake of the Woods border with Canada. His dad was Billy Christian, star of the 1960 US team that won the first Gold Medal at Squaw Valley, California, and his uncle, Roger, was on the same team. Another uncle, Gordon, played on the 1956 US Olympic team. A quick, clever scorer at center or wing at the University of North Dakota, and later during a 15-year NHL career, Christian was converted to defense for the 1980 team by Brooks, who valued puck-rushing defensemen to bolster the offense. He contributed numerous key plays, including three assists against West Germany when the US overcame a 2–0 deficit, and the key assist on Mark Johnson's goal in the final second of the first period against the USSR. Right after the 1980 Olympics, he signed with the Winnipeg Jets, scoring a goal seven seconds into his first game and becoming captain at age 22. He played four years with the Jets, seven years with the Washington Capitals, two with the Boston Bruins, and parts of two more with the Chicago Blackhawks, totaling 340 goals and 433 assists in 1,009 career games. He reached the Stanley Cup Finals in 1990 with Boston and was named to the 1991 NHL All-Star Game. He also played on the US teams in the 1981, 1984, and 1991 Canada Cup tournaments and at the 1981 and 1989 World Championships. After leaving hockey, he worked as a developmental group leader for Cardinal Glass, in its Fargo, North Dakota, office.

25. Buzzy Schneider, left winger, born in Grand Rapids, Michigan, grew up and played high school hockey at Babbitt, Minnesota, was nicknamed the "Babbitt Rabbit" for his speed, played on 1974 Minnesota NCAA championship team, then scored 39–31–70 during the 1976 US Olympic team season and played in the IHL at Milwaukee for two seasons before making the 1980 US team. Left wing on the "Conehead Line," Schneider scored 5–3–8 in the seven Olympic games, including two goals against Czechoslovakia, two against Romania, and the first US goal against the USSR in the "miracle" medal-round victory. After 1980, he played in Switzerland and played for the US in the 1982 World Championships. He was portrayed by his son, Billy, in the movie *Miracle*, who played high school hockey at Twin Cities suburban Mounds View. After hockey, Buzzy made a career in real estate.

27. Phil Verchota, left winger, Duluth, Minnesota, played on the 1976 and 1979 Gophers NCAA championship teams coached by Herb Brooks, who sought the 6-foot-2, hard-charging competitor for the 1979 US National team at the World Championships and the 1980 Team USA. He scored three goals in the seven Olympic games, including a goal early in the third period that tied the game, 2–2, and inspired the three-goal rally against Finland. Played in Finland after the 1980 games, was on the 1982 US National team, and captained the 1984 US Olympic team. Went into the banking business and became president of the Bemidji, Minnesota, branch of the Deerwood Bank group.

28. John Harrington, Virginia, Minnesota, right wing on the Conehead Line with center Mark Pavelich, a teammate and linemate at Minnesota-Duluth, kept a notebook file of "Brooksisms," the coach's oft-repeated clichés, fractured and otherwise. Went on to play minor league pro hockey and in Europe and played on the 1984 US Olympic team before going into coaching. A serious student of the game, he was an assistant coach at Denver and at St. Cloud State before getting the chance to be head coach at St. John's, a Division III private college near St. Cloud, where his teams thrived on his imaginative techniques and won five Minnesota Intercollegiate Athletic Conference titles and made five NCAA D-III appearances. He left St. John's to coach in Switzerland and Italy and the Slovenian National team before becoming Division I women's coach at Minnesota State-Mankato in the dominant WCHA.

30. Jim Craig, Easton, Massachusetts, goaltender from Boston University, where he backstopped the Terriers to the 1978 NCAA championship, and his play on the US team at the 1979 World Championships for Herb Brooks convinced the US coach he would be a consistent presence and competitor in goal on the 1980 team. He had some shaky starts to several games, contributing to the US giving up the first goal in six of their seven Olympic games, but he seemed to grow steadier as each game went on, while his teammates rallied to go 6–0–1. He stopped 36 shots in the 4–3 victory over the USSR in the "Miracle" game, and after the US won, Craig spun away from his teammates and skated over toward the boards. A fan threw him an American flag, and he unfolded it and wrapped it around his shoulders while he continued to seek out and locate his father in the jubilant crowd. That flag was later displayed at the Sports Museum of America in New York City, before it closed in 2009. After the Olympics, Craig signed with the Atlanta Flames and won his first game but never recaptured the magic he had at Lake Placid. He played briefly for Boston as a backup, and for the US in the 1983 B Pool world tournament, but retired in 1984 after a brief try with the Minnesota North Stars. He has continued to make motivational speaking engagements and is president of Gold Medal Strategies in Boston.

Brooks was always loyal to his most trusted aides, and it was at his insistence that Dr. V. George Nagobads, Trainer Gary Smith, goalie coach Warren Strelow, and training guru Jack Blatherwick all accompanied Team USA. Blatherwick's later influence on NHL teams and USA Hockey resulted in him receiving the 2019 Lester Patrick Award.

The assorted and diverse personalities of the Team USA players has scattered them all in different directions, with some of them—most notably Mike Ramsey, Mark Johnson, Ken Morrow, and John Harrington—remaining in hockey for long careers in coaching or administration. There continue to be occasions to come together, for meaningful reunions or special tributes. And on those occasions, they all realize that they are joined forever by the family bond of the unique Team USA of 1980.